A COOPERATIVE METHOD
OF
LEARNING LOGIC AND ANALYSIS
IN GENEALOGY

The Power of Truth, Evidence, and Analytical Thinking

William M. Litchman, Ph.D.

HERITAGE BOOKS
2017

HERITAGE BOOKS

AN IMPRINT OF HERITAGE BOOKS, INC.

Books, CDs, and more—Worldwide

For our listing of thousands of titles see our website
at
www.HeritageBooks.com

Published 2017 by
HERITAGE BOOKS, INC.
Publishing Division
5810 Ruatan Street
Berwyn Heights, Md. 20740

International Standard Book Number
Paperbound: 978-0-7884-5783-8

Table of Contents

Preface

Logic, Analysis, and Rational Thinking in Genealogical Research

No matter who you are, the way you think is quite your own. Your history, your family, your education, your experiences, all add to the creation of the way you think. In fact, it is almost impossible for someone to consciously get outside of themselves to get a picture of what others see. Our own reactions to our surroundings are unique, biased, and slanted, tilted to a degree that is all our own.

So, to teach someone how to think is an almost impossible task. This is what a university education is all about. For someone to judge what approach to take to shift that unique mental construct that is us is not something that can be done with ease and to set up protocols which will work with even a small fraction of our population just can't happen. I'm not recommending to you that you embark on four years of university education in order to acquire a different way of thinking (though it really wouldn't hurt). Most of us simply don't have the time, energy, or funds to do this at our time of life (no matter what that is).

The crunch really comes when we have finished the beginnings of our family research in which we've interviewed, scoured our home and taken on faith all of the family stories for which we searched and constructed our family tree. That tree is the beginning or our own downfall because we believe in it implicitly. After all, our own grandfather lived through the times he tells us about and how could his stories be even slightly off-kilter?

As soon as we begin to move outside our comfort zone in exploring our family and find public documents relating to family members who have been mentioned or shown to us but whom we have never known or met, then we begin to find that not everything in our berry patch is ripe for the picking. We find that there are dead ends, partial truths, incomplete stories and even conflicting bits of evidence which we now have to explain and fit together.

To do this explaining will require honesty, truth-finding, and skill in putting together a family picture created from only partial pieces, innuendo, and inference. In fact, to move further outward from ourselves into this unknown place where we don't have a firm idea of what is fact and what is fancy, we now begin to realize the value of rational thinking, based on logic and analysis, and critical examination of the evidence we've found.

Logic is a science that deals with the principles and criteria governing correct or reliable inference.[1] It is important to use reasonable arguments based on good judgment. The

---

[1] https://www.merriam-webster.com/dictionary/logic ; http://www.dictionary.com/browse/logic.

result of the application of logic should not only be reasonable but correct. Analysis is the process of breaking a complex whole into its simpler constituent parts. It is the opposite of synthesis. The result of analysis is a means to understanding the complexity of people's lives, families, relationships, and decisions. These principles are applied to the evidence gathered to reach a goal or solve a problem. Complex genealogical research problems are solved by the application of the rules and principles of logic and analysis coupled with rational thinking and inference.

Knowing where to look for evidence is one of the things that teachers, lecturers, and mentors can show us how to do. There are experts in all sorts of documentary sources, common and otherwise, and they can tell us precisely where they are, what we should expect them to hold for us, and how we can access them. We can find experts on specific repositories and experts on the documents relating to specific geographical places. So gathering evidence is not really the problem that we face when it comes to trying to build another generation of our family.

In fact, we can gather in much more evidence than we often know what to do with while exploring our family. What happens, for example, when we find two documents which present the birth of an ancestor and they don't agree. Both appear to be genuine, contemporary, and highly reliable and yet they say two different things.

What can we do to make judgments about which document to believe and which one to disregard. Of course, we hate to throw out anything that has taken us so long to find in the first place, but there can't be two birth dates for the same person … can there?

To solve many of these conundrums and to be able to move forward with confidence with our research when we don't have the full picture, we must be able to apply our ability to fit bits and pieces of indirect evidence from many disparate sources together into a coherent whole which will satisfy the proof standard for genealogy. These skills come unnaturally to many because our training and experience haven't allowed us to practice using our brain in those ways. Because of our unique nature, there isn't any single remedy for us to apply which will guarantee success and the proofs we need.

So, how do we proceed to gain understanding, and the ability to use logic and analysis like an expert genealogist?

When I was young, my father told me stories of his family, which had lived in Marblehead, Massachusetts, for several generations. The story of his family coming to Marblehead was an exciting one to a Kansas boy.

In late fall of 1833, Dad's great-great-grandfather Thomas Lishman, deserting his wife and five children in Newfoundland, took his eight-year-old son William and walked across the island on which he lived to find a fishing vessel packing their catch into the hold. He made an arrangement with John Russell, the captain of *The Mechanic*, to work for his passage for himself and his son to Marblehead, their home port. There, Thomas apprenticed William to a shoemaker, and then joined a fishing crew in Gloucester. He returned in 1838, changed his son's apprenticeship, and departed once more, this time for good.

After his second apprenticeship, William decided to be a fisherman. In 1845, his girl friend, Sarah Bartlett, warned him of the dangers of that occupation. That same year, most of Marblehead's fishing fleet was lost in a violent storm at sea. William changed his surname to Litchman, married Sarah, and settled down to shoemaking.

In the spring of 1883, after fifty years away from his Newfoundland roots, William Litchman read the newspaper account of a Gloucester fishing dory that had recently gotten lost from its mother ship, *The Grace L. Fears*, on the Grand Banks. The fisherman, Howard Blackburn, rowed 60 miles in freezing weather to the barren south coast of Newfoundland, where the family of Francis Lishman rescued and cared for him. William, recognizing the familiar name, wrote to the Lishmans. He soon got an answer from his long-lost Lishman brother, and after a reunion in NF, they stayed in contact for the rest of William's life.

These tales of a man's experience on the ocean and William's reunion with his family sparked a life-long interest in family history for me.

Because of severe asthma, I had to leave my Kansas home when I was fifteen and live with my maternal grandfather in Colorado. In poking around his attic, I found several dusty, long-forgotten boxes of photographs, letters, and diaries, including a small, home-made handwritten book describing the Irish family of my long-deceased grandmother's great-grandparents. The book detailed the births, marriages, and deaths of this couple's fifteen children, including those still-born, and told the story of their trip from Londonderry, Ireland, by the ship *Tristram* to Philadelphia in May 1792.

In 1956, upon graduation from high school, I gathered this family material together, and took it with me to my dormitory at the university. The summer following my freshman year saw the death of my grandfather and the quick emptying and sale of his home. Had I not "acquired" this unique and valuable family collection, it would have been lost completely and finally. My mother was greatly relieved when she asked me, many years later, what happened to all that "stuff."

As I studied to become a chemist, I learned the basic rules of scientific enquiry: planning experiments, controlling experimental variables, and, especially, making observations. A particularly nice thing about this background is that experiences in scientific experimentation apply also to family-history research.

Later (1985), I wrote to "any Lishman family" in Grey River, Newfoundland, which was called Little River when my great-great grandfather reunited with his family. A letter came back to me from Ruby Lushman (the current spelling of the family name), who proved to be a fourth cousin of mine, both of us having descended from that same Thomas Lishman (and his wife, Susannah McDonald) who left with his son in 1833. Ruby, too, remembered the famous story of Howard Blackburn and his extraordinary courage and dogged persistence in surviving, with the help of the Lishmans.

These experiences have fueled my fascination with family history research and helped me make great strides in self-taught genealogy, during a time when this field was still governed by letter-writing, travel to remote cemeteries, and dependence upon the great kindnesses of family members in sharing what they knew.

While you may not have had the advantage of scientific training in your life, the skills of logical and analytical thinking so basic to science and to genealogy can be yours. In a life-time of teaching, I have found ways to help others build the skills needed to provide believable proof for conclusions based only on indirect and limited evidence. These skills are accessible to you and to all who have the desire, dedication, and persistence to learn to think rationally, using logic and analysis to work through proofs where evidence is fragmentary and piece-meal.

Follow the learning path outlined in Chapter 1, and use real-life examples of how logic and rational thinking leads to solving tricky family-history problems. Use the method outlined there to develop your abilities and skills for finding solutions in genealogical research. It is all right to work alone on this but it is much better to assemble a discussion group of people who want to learn together. Two of you or up to a dozen, the input from other minds will help you.

Chapter 1

Learning Observation, Analysis, and Logic
for Your Genealogical Research[1]

Sherlock Holmes uses scientific methods. When pursuing his criminals, He constantly observes. He dashes from place to place, looking through his magnifying glass. He picks up cigar ash, fingerprints, and bits of glass, gathering his clues. And then he sits back in his chair to analyze the data he has gathered, before he astounds the police, Dr. Watson, and his admirers with his genius.

It is the chase that keeps up the interest, homing in on the elusive criminal as he twists and turns desperately, trying to escape the clutches of the master detective. But try as he might, it is impossible to get away from the mind like a steel trap which stays focused on the trail, using every clue, combining them into a net so tight and so secure that no matter what he does, the criminal eventually succumbs to the iron grasp of the law.

The gathering of information is one of the things that both detectives and genealogists do very well. Genealogists diligently search an extensive range of document sources (church, census, probate, vital, military, and immigration records, deeds and land records, newspapers and magazines, etc.) for clues to their family history.

But analysis and logic are at the root of all successful criminal or genealogical detective stories and yet most introductory research courses touch only lightly on this aspect of research. We are taught about the research process and then the remainder of the time, sometimes as much as ninety percent of the course deals with the several classes of document groups (census, probate, deeds, etc). Even advanced courses, conferences, and seminars simply dig deeper into documents, perhaps concentrating on more obscure types of documents, new or unusual classes of them, or new locations for and subtle variations on the finding of evidence.

Knowledge of document sources is not bad, certainly it is essential, but it is not everything. This exclusive approach to the teaching of genealogy makes the student feel that "if I don't find something on my family history in this source, then it isn't worth my reading it."

Courses which move beyond the mere study of sources and into the implementation

---

[1] Based on an article by William M Litchman, NGS News Magazine, Vol 26, #6, Nov/Dec, 2000, pp 340-343.

of logic and analysis are rare. It is more difficult to teach the skills of analysis and logic. However, most of the changes occurring in genealogical standards and family history research don't lie in the document sources but in how they are used. Acquisition of evidence, as important as that is, is only a part of successful problem solving. Analytical thinking, and the successful structure-building which produces genealogical "proof," are at least as important. The elusive ancestor must be entrapped in the iron net forged through the logical use of evidence.

On completion of a basic course, one student said, "When I first became interested in genealogy, almost all of my older relatives were no longer around to answer questions about their ancestors. As with any other novice; I was told to start with myself, what I knew factually about my immediate family, and work backwards. I quickly exhausted the "easy" sources: local newspapers, the federal census, family bible, letters, etc. The local Family History Center volunteers were extremely helpful in providing advice on available microfilmed documents. Acknowledging I needed additional instruction in methodology, I then took a short course in basic genealogy. This was helpful but there was no real world experience. I took the intermediate course and advanced seminar because the attendees discuss and study what someone actually accomplished and published."

Broadening our reading interests beyond studies dealing with our surname is of great value to individual genealogists (at all levels) as well as the community at large. Realizing that any community of genealogists can better thrive and progress if opportunities for advanced discussion and learning are available, a group of interested people decided to move from the typical beginning research course and the more advanced discussions of document groups to deeper discussions of logic, analysis, and the use of evidence.

This discussion group showed a desire to know more about the importance of evidence and how it can be used effectively. It appeared that a seminar format would be the very best way to provide a stimulating and guided discussion series where the instructor could guide the conversation without appearing to be overbearing.

In order to approach these more difficult skills, set up an intermediate discussion course consisting of a series of eight or more two-hour discussions to analytically read and study a series of eight or more articles published in recent issues of a peer-reviewed genealogical journal such as the *National Genealogical Society Quarterly*. This journal is peer-reviewed and the subject matter addressed includes research techniques and methodology. Use some care in the selection of the articles although almost all of the articles in this journal will qualify for the seminar's attention.

Each student was asked to read each paper in the series at least four times before coming to the discussion meeting. None of the articles chosen for the series dealt directly with any of the students' current surname interests. It is important to choose the series in advance to fit this standard. The first reading was simply to acquaint the student with the overall picture of the problem. The second was to include a careful reading of the general argument or problem including the footnotes. A third reading was meant to fully understand the evidence and to track the logic used in solving the problem. The fourth reading is to make sure that the details of the arguments and logic are correct, sound, and successful, taking great care with an eye to detail.

As each paper is read, it is important to note the acquisition of evidence and the almost unconscious use of the skills of grading sources to realize which ones are unbiased, independent, and truthful in representing the facts which appear to be useful in connection with the problem to be solved. While source documents of lower quality shouldn't be thrown away with the bath-water, when conflicts arise within the evidence, knowing which bits to trust implicitly and which to suspect is a valuable asset in the analytical process.

Sometimes, looking again at evidence we have been staring at requires leaving it aside for a time and going back again with fresh eyes. Sometimes, just thinking a bit "outside the play-pen" will give a new view of what was seen before. This same idea can apply to the reading of the series of papers. It may not be obvious what the author has done until you are familiar enough with the problem and its solution to envision the pathway from one to the other.

Learn as you go, adding more and more to your valuable data base of operational techniques and useful ideas. Especially important is remembering that unexpected results for a science experiment signal an important clue in understanding "how things work." If an experiment gives a "wrong" result, carefully repeating the experimental conditions many times show whether the result is really wrong or whether the theoretical understanding of "how things work" is wrong.

It's always important to be prepared to accept all of the data rather than picking only those things which bear up our theories. We never learn if we bias our results; let's be honest and truthful in our observations and reportings.

Each discussion was lead by the moderator (teacher) but was an open and unbiased discussion of the subject article of the seminar. The point of each discussion was the use of analysis and logic rather than simply finding evidence. That is, the students were reading these articles without the motive of advancing their own specific evidence needs. There need be no exams or quizzes throughout the course and no one should be ridiculed for proposing ideas to the discussion.

Some comments by the students in one seminar are instructive. Many of these students were neophyte genealogists when they took their first basic research course and were joined by more experienced researchers as they continued to the intermediate class.

As one commented: "The … class before it had been excellent and in that group we had begun to analyze and share many ideas beyond our class reading assignments. They were tremendously stimulating conversations that naturally led to wanting to do and learn more in analytical readings and genealogical writings."

Another valued the group input in analysing different approaches to research: "The first thing I realized is that I had forgotten how to read an article and be able to discuss it intelligently. The articles assigned were written to instruct as well as provide family histories. The techniques used by experts were sometimes ingenious. I was impressed with the amount of time and effort some authors took to solve a problem. The procedure to get to a conclusion was not direct and clues were found in places I would not ordinarily look."

Then, as the group matured in their analytical skills and the depth of their discussions of logic and analysis, our advanced seminar in research and genealogical writing was created. The seminar format is used here (as opposed to a "course") because while there is a moderator, each student has the opportunity to be the leader. The group decided that they would continue to meet and discuss the periodical literature but that if any in the group had the courage to organize and present their own genealogical research, then the group would use their newly acquired skills of analytical reading to discuss their own work.

"Initially, I did not plan to attend the advanced seminar because I lacked research experience to write a genealogical article," said one participant.

At the outset, this requires a deal of courage on the part of the participants who had never published any of their own work, nor whom had even considered doing so. Several of the group were determined not to make an attempt at writing but one or two were willing to give it a try as long as the rest of the group would be kind to them in their criticism and analysis. If no student-produced paper was available at the time of the seminar, then the analytical reading of published works would continue as it had in the past.

As the course progressed the participants made discoveries about both the craft of writing and its value in enhancing research.

"Humility isn't exactly sweet tasting!" said one participant. "Exploring writing is hard but well-worth pursuing. It is a craft that can be learned with lots and lots of practice and more rewriting."

"On several occasions [it had been] emphasized how the actual process of writing an article would compel us to focus on the genealogical problem at hand. Focus indeed!! Stating the genealogical problem, analyzing the information and presenting it in a manner for a reader to easily follow becomes a monumental task. My attempt to write an article has made me aware of many problems I did not know existed in my research. I know what I mean, but others would soon be lost..."

One of the strongest positive aspects to this approach to learning advanced group support techniques is that (as one participant said), "the seminar participants consist of a group of supportive individuals who are eager to sharpen their research skills. The noncompetitive nature of the group couples with the skill and demeanor of the facilitator provide a pleasant environment [for] learning and sharing the peculiarities of slave research."

It cannot be overemphasized that the support of class members for each other is essential to the success of any endeavor such as this. Another mentioned, "... I immediately felt at home with the informal, congenial, constructive, and encouraging atmosphere of the group. I found that some people in the group were highly motivated to write their family histories for publication while others, like myself, were more interested in learning new approaches and advanced techniques of research that emerges from writing and critiquing both published and unpublished articles. Soon, it was apparent that I, too, should attempt to write an article in order to profit from the group's ideas on how I could improve my research..."

It is important to note that five articles have been produced in a group consisting of ten members, something almost unimaginable at the start. As stated by the participants: "I have always held National Genealogical Society articles in high esteem; however, I certainly now read them at a whole different level due to the exercise of analyzing the methodology of those articles in class. My research techniques [i.e. evidence gathering] have not changed all that much; however, my analysis of the data found has improved and I want to continue writing as I have found it to be a wonderful way to see problems more clearly."

"Instead of scattering my efforts in searching for clues on a myriad of ancestors at once, I now identify a specific problem and focus my attention on it. This particular method has proven to be a much better utilization of my time."

"The advanced seminar was designed to put into practice techniques of experienced genealogists. The process of writing a problem … clearly shows one where more research needs to be done. [It] … is not as simple as may be expected. I would rather have the seminar class critique my paper and be able to take advantage of their comments than to send it to a publisher and be completely demoralized after one attempt."

"I'm more critical of sources and published material which can take a lot of effort to correct. I'm more confident of my opinion as far as evaluating material."

" I have learned to appreciate the rewards of tenacity and the importance of focus. I have also learned the importance of clarity and specificity in annotating citations. I … have learned to appreciate the worth of my slave ancestry research. As a result, I have produced an article proving an aspect of my family's oral history."

In general, the feelings of the students have been positive, supportive, desiring success, and helping the other students feel successful and, overall, this has been the result of the group's efforts. To put it into a nutshell, one student concluded: "I would like to have this seminar continue."

This book presents a series of researched problems. Some have been previously published and others are fresh to this presentation. Additional problems for continuing study can easily be found in any of several high-quality journals such as *The National Genealogical Society Quarterly, The American Genealogist, The New York Genealogical and Biographical Record, The Genealogist, The New England Historic Genealogical Record, Journal of Family History, Genealogy, The Journal of Genealogy and Family History*, and others. It is important to choose reading material from sources which use peer-review techniques to vet their material prior to publication.

The process of gaining understanding and skill in the application of logic and analysis is to read the real-life cases which others have solved using these techniques. Reading the explanation of the proof arguments and the evidence and logic which was used to construct them will open this world of rational thinking to each of us. The recipe for success is explained below.

It is up to you and your own circumstances as to whether a collaborative group can gather with you to pursue this goal. Having a mentor is also not required though may be helpful. Choosing one of the group to be the mentor is a possibility or rotate the leadership from meeting to meeting. Having more than one mind to bounce ideas against is a very useful tool. Care should be taken to be positive, kind, and caring throughout the meetings. Feelings are important.

Chapter 2

The Case of the Missing Grandma:
The Mysterious Mother of William Burke Cline

Memories can quickly fade with the passing of time. If family stories and exploits aren't told and retold, they will be lost. It's understandable that embarrassing or painful episodes might be quickly brushed under the rug but even exciting stories from the past can soon be lost if not told around the family camp fire.

This problem begins with memories of a child of such a family faded by nearly 70 years of time. The father of the family, William Burke Cline, an Amarillo stockman born in Omaha, died in an airplane crash shortly before the birth, in November 1949, of his second child.[1] His wife was named Phyllis and his first child was born about 1942. After serving in World War II, William's premature death was so traumatic and painful that the family refrained from speaking to the children about him or his family. Grandpa Cline, William Samuel, was the only member of William Burke's family known to the children.

– Under what circumstances did the crash happen?

– Who is grandma Cline, mother of William Burke Cline?

From what is known, the crash must have happened between February and November 1949. Failing to find any mention of an airplane crash in available Amarillo papers, further searching is necessary. William Burke Cline's mother was mentioned by William Samuel when he filed his World War I draft registration card saying he was "single (wife dead)."[2] Subsequently, William Burke (age 4 yrs, 11 mos) was living in Omaha with his father and his second wife, Augusta.[3] Ten years later he was living (at age 15) in Omaha with his aunt Nora and her husband Earl J. Burke.[4]

When in high school, William B. Cline was involved in an accident in which another young man was seriously injured. Virgil Williams, riding a motorcycle, was the same age as William, both 17 years old. Virgil's skull was fractured and William was charged with

---

[1]   Story told by a member of the Cline family to the author.

[2]   *U.S., World War I Draft Registration Cards, 1917-1918*, (Ancestry), Roll 1711761, draft board 4, 5 Jun 1917.

[3]   William S. Cline household, *1920 federal census*, T625, Roll 989, p 12, ED 70, sheet 12A, lines 51-55, 3819 S 20th St., ward 7, Omaha, Douglas, Nebraska, dwelling 236, family 244. (Ancestry)

[4]   Earl J. Burke household, *1930 federal census*, T626, Roll 1276, p 211, ED 28-159, sheet 38A, lines 25-30, 4902 Walnut St, ward 8, Omaha, Douglas, Nebraska, dwelling 474, family 475. (Ancestry)

reckless driving.[5]

He attended the University of Nebraska in Lincoln,[6] graduating from there in 1937[7] but because of the great depression, he had to support himself in the Civilian Conservation Corps in Bismarck, Nebraska.[8] He married Phyllis Althea Johnson, 27 January 1941.[9]

He served in the U.S. Army Air Service having joined from the University of Nebraska with the rank of Second Lieutenant.[10] He was temporarily promoted from Captain to Major in 1943.[11] Right at the end of the war, he was again promoted, this time from Major to Lieutenant Colonel in which it stated: "the colonel was commissioned a second lieutenant from the reserves at the University of Nebraska in June, 1937. He went to Fort Ord, California, with the 17th Infantry in 1940. Colonel Cline entered flying school and received his wings in September, 1942."[12]

An announcement in the *Omaha World-Herald* declared his death in a plane crash. "A former Omahan was one of two men killed in a light plane crash near Waynoka, Okla, the International News Service reported Friday." Waynoka is a city in Woods county, population 927, about 4 miles north of Little Sahara State Park. "The dead men were W B (Bill) Cline, Jr, about 34, Amarillo, Tex, cattle man who was born and raised in Omaha and J W McBrayer, rancher of White Deer, Tex. The two had been missing since September 8, when they left Omaha on their way back to Amarillo, in Mr McBrayer's plane. They refueled that day at Hill City, Kans, planned to fly by way of Salina and Wichita, Kans, to avoid bad weather. The wrecked airplane was found Thursday seven miles southwest of Waynoka. Mr Cline, a South High and University of Nebraska graduate, was a veteran pilot. During World War II, he was a lieutenant colonel on the Inspector General's staff in England. Besides his parents, he is survived by his wife, Phyllis, and a daughter, Susan."[13] Susan was born circa 1942.[14]

The article doesn't mention that Phyllis Cline was pregnant at the time of his death and subsequently gave birth to her second child two months after his body was discovered.

---

[5]   *Omaha World-Herald*, Wednesday, 2 November 1932, p 1. "North High Boy Critically Hurt in Cycle Crash." **http://www.genealogybank.com/**

[6]   *Lincoln Evening Journal*, Monday, 5 February 1934, p 7, col 1. **http://www.genealogybank.com/**

[7]   *US, School Yearbooks, 1880-2012* (Ancestry), 1935, Delta Tau Delta pledge; 1936-7, member of Delta Tau Delta fraternity.

[8]   William B. Cline household, *1940 federal census*, T627, Roll 2261, p 9A, ED 71-2, sheet 1A, line 1, Civilian Conxervation Corps SCS 18, Bismarck, Platte, Nebraska, dwelling and family blank. (Ancestry)

[9]   *The Nebraska State Journal* (Lincoln), 21 Jan 1941, Tue, p 5, col 2, "Johnson-Cline." Also appeared in the *Lincoln Evening Journal*, 20 Jan 1941, p 5, col 2; and *The Lincoln Star*, 20 Jan 1941, p. 7. *The Lincoln Star*, Monday, 27 Jan 1941, p 7, col 4. "Number of Midwinter Nuptial Ceremonies, Johnson-Cline." (Ancestry)

[10]   *Omaha World-Herald*, Sunday, 19 January 1941, p 79, cols 6-7. "Miss Johnson to Wed Omahan." **http://www.genealogybank.com/**

[11]   *The Nebraska State Journal* (Lincoln), Monday, 11 Oct 1943, p 1, col 7 (Ancestry).

[12]   *The Amarillo Globe-Times*, Thursday, 10 May 1945, p 11, col 1. *The Amarillo Globe-Times*, Tuesday, 15 May 1945, p 6, col 2. **http://www.genealogybank.com/**

[13]   *Omaha World-Herald*, Friday, 16 Sep 1949, p 25, "Ex-Omahan Died in Plane Crash." **http://www.genealogybank.com/**

[14]   Information supplied by Susan's sister.

A second article in the *Dallas Morning News* gave a few more details: "Texas Fliers' Bodies Found. Amarillo, Texas, Sept. 15 (AP). The bodies of two flying Texas cattlemen were found Thursday in the charred wreckage of their plane in rugged Oklahoma hill country. William B Cline, 32, Amarillo cattleman, and J W McBrayer, White Deer rancher, were found burned beyond recognition. An Air Force rescue plane first spotted the missing craft on a hillside seven miles southwest of Waynoka, Okla. The rescue plane dropped five parachutists, equipped with medical supplies and 2-way radios. By radio the parachutists directed Sheriff W S Gillen Jr of Oklahoma to the scene. The crash site was inaccessible by car and one and a half miles from a highway. The bodies had to be carried out to where a Waynoka ambulance waited. Cline and McBrayer were returning to Texas last week from the Cleveland air races. The last word from them was as they passed over Wichita, Kan., last Thursday. They radioed for a report of weather conditions near Gage, Okla., and Amarillo."[15]

So, it is fairly clear that they were concerned about the weather in their flight path home to Amarillo. It is possible they encountered turbulence and a thunderstorm which brought them down. The weather reports in the newspapers of the time reported mild, sunny to partly cloudy conditions over the entire Nebraska, Iowa, and Kansas region: calm winds, scattered thundershowers, and daytime temperatures in the mid to upper 70s.[16] It is very likely that these two experienced pilots were caught in a thunderstorm which forced their craft into the ground. These sources give the circumstances surrounding the death of William Burke Cline in an airplane crash.

William's father survived through four marriages[17] and a gun battle in an Amarillo hotel which nearly cost him his life,[18] but there is no evidence yet of the name of William Burke's mother.

In an announcement of promotion for William Burke Cline,[19] his *grandparents* are named. Mr. and Mrs. J. M. Eller of 2817 N. 20th St., Omaha, must have been his maternal grandparents since their name is Eller, not Cline.

Reasoning that they might have been living in Omaha for quite a number of years, a search was made for this couple. They were found living at that same address with their son, Clyde, age 36.[20] William Burke's mother was dead by 1917 but was probably living with

---

[15]   *Dallas Morning News*, Friday, 16 Sep 1949, p 21. "Texas Fliers' Bodies Found."
http://www.genealogybank.com/

[16]   *The Nebraska State Journal* (Lincoln, Neb), Friday 8 September 1949, p 1, col 1. (Ancestry)

[17]   Marriage number one is the one sought. Marriage number two is apparent from the 1920 census, above. Marriage number three is found in *Iowa, Marriage Records, 1880-1937* (Ancestry): to Lonita Hunt, 16 Mar 1924, Glenwood Mills, Iowa. Marriage number four is to Evelyn Gobel, daughter of Louis A. Gobel, *Omaha World-Herald*, Tuesday, 9 April 1957, p 16. (Ancestry)

[18]   *Omaha World-Herald*, Saturday, 31 Mar 1934, p 1: "Omaha Man Kills Foe Who Wounds Him in Gun Duel. W. S. Cline Shot After Quarrel Over Cattle Deal." *Omaha World-Herald Evening*, Saturday, 31 Mar 1934, p 1: "W S Cline Wounded, Opponent is Slain." *Omaha World-Herald*, Monday 2 Apr 1934, p 1, "Cline's Condition Remains Critical." *Omaha World-Herald*, Tuesday 3 Apr 1934, p 1, "Cline Near Crisis, His Doctor Reports."
http://www.genealogybank.com/

[19]   *Omaha World-Herald*, Thursday, 3 May 1945, p 21. http://www.genealogybank.com/

[20]   J. M. Eller household, *1920 federal census*, T625, Roll 987, p 269, ED 19, sheet 12A, lines 3-5, 2817 N 20th St, Omaha, Douglas, Nebraska, dwelling 237, family 482. (Ancestry)

her family before her marriage. The family was found at 2413 N. 24th St, Omaha, with two children, Clyde, age 25 and Genevieve A., age 16.[21] Clara, Genevieve's mother, married once, claimed only two children born to her and both were living at the time. She claimed the same in 1900 when Genevieve A. was 6 years old, born Nov 1893 and her brother, Clyde, was age 16, b Sep 1886, living at 2025 Spruce St, Omaha.[22] Joshua's father-in-law, Frederick Buck (age 91) and his sister-in-law, Ava Grace Buck (age 44) were both living with the family at that time. Buck is apparently Clara's maiden name.

A search of local Omaha newspapers revealed only one mention of Genevieve[23] and none of William Burke Cline's birth. City directories failed to list the spouse of William S Cline though his name is prominent through the years between 1915 and 1920. A burial record for Genevieve (Eller) Cline is found at the Forest Lawn Memorial Park in Omaha. Her tombstone reads "Genevieve Eller Cline, 1893-1916,"[24] suggesting that she died over a year after William's birth.[25]

Ordinarily vital records would be documents of choice to solve this problem but Nebraska's laws regarding vital records are so restrictive[26] that none of the living family qualify to obtain a copy of the birth, marriage, or death records for William Samuel Cline or Genevieve A. (Eller) Cline. Applying for the only birth record for William Burke Cline got the response "no record."[27]

Even without that record, the evidence documented here conclusively shows that Genevieve A. Eller is the first wife of William S Cline and mother of William Burke Cline. The missing grandma is found!

---

[21]   Joshua M Eller household, *1910 federal census*, T624, Roll 843, p 134B-135A, ED 39, sheet 2B-3A, lines 99-100, 1-4, 2232 N 24th St., Omaha, Douglas, Nebraska, dwelling 43, family 50. (Ancestry)

[22]   Joshua Ellen household, *1900 federal census*, T623, Roll 924, p 168B, ED 69, sheet 12B, lines 69-72, 2025 Spruce St, Omaha, Douglas, Nebraska, dwelling 241, family 266. (Ancestry)

[23]   *Evening World Herald*, Sunday, 19 September, 1909, p 15, col 3, "... Miss Genevieve Eller, pianist ...". http://www.genealogybank.com/

[24]   http://www.findagrave.com/ memorial #37003308.

[25]   Perhaps during pregnancy for a second birth.

[26]   A legal copy of a birth, marriage, death, stillbirth, or divorce certificates cannot be issued without *proper purpose*. A person may obtain a certificate for self, spouse, parent, or child. See http://dhhs.ne.gov/Pages/default.aspx.

[27]   Letter from the DHHS Office of Vital Records, PO Box 95065, Lincoln, NE "Searched all of NE indexes 1912-2017." Result was no record.

Chapter 3

Using Passenger Lists to Find a Woman's Maiden Name[1]

Background

A method of finding a woman's maiden name was discovered while researching a Jewish family, victims of the November 9, 1938 Hamburg pogrom.

Simon Bogopolsky, a business man in Hamburg, born circa 1897, Odessa, Ukraine, married a woman named Erna (maiden name unknown); born circa 1907, Berlin, prior to his leaving Germany with their two children.[2] Their exit from Germany was hastened by rough treatment by the Brown Shirts of Nazi tyranny, which devasted the lives and property of Jews throughout the reach of that government.

What was Erna's maiden name?

Simon Bogopolsky is the son of Boris and Bella (Orlof) Bogopolsky.[3] He moved to München with his parents, thence to Wiesbaden (1930-32) where he established a leather goods business,[4] and then to Hamburg (1932-37)[5] where he married and where his two sons, Boris (b circa 1932) and Renate (b circa 1935) were born.

With the loss of their business, Simon and Erna arranged to escape to the United States and freedom. Their names on a passenger list for their arrival in New York, show them with their children. They departed from Southampton, England, on the ship *President Roosevelt*, on 23 December 1938, and arrived at New York on New Year's Eve.[6] In that passenger list, Simon claims that their nearest relative in their home country is his mother-in-law, Mrs. Helene Aberbach of 42 Rimska, Praha XII, Czechoslovakia. His wife, Erna, claims this person as her mother and the grandmother of her children. The name was originally typed as "Mrs Aberbaum" but typed over as "Mrs Helene Aberbach." Two different

---

[1]   Permission to use this problem was given by Roni Stern, 3 April 2017.

[2]   Simon Bogoposk household, *1940 federal census*, T627, Roll 2674, p 24903, ED 31-2026, sheet 1A, lines 27-31, 620 west 190th st, New York, New York, New York, enumerated 2 April 1940 by Harry H Unger, family 9. (Ancestry).

[3]   Hand-written note by Ron Stern, 25 February 2016, grand-nephew of Simon Bogopolsky.

[4]   *Deutsche Telefonbücher, 1915-1981* (Ancestry.com.de), 1930-1932.

[5]   *Ibid.* 1932-37.

[6]   *New York, Passenger Lists, 1820-1957* (Ancestry.com), Year: 1938; Arrival: New York, New York; Microfilm Serial: T715, 1897-1957; Microfilm Roll: Roll 6267; Line: 6; Page Number: 159.

typewriters were used having obviously different fonts. It is not clear which name is accurate or correct, if either. Simon and Erna intended to join Simon's nephew, Mr Sam Orlow (alternate spelling of Orlof), 111 West 89th Street, New York.

Steps to a solution

A further search of the collected passenger lists for the port of New York revealed two additional passenger lists containing Bogopolsky names of interest. One was for Julian Aberbach (arr 21 July 1939),[7] who claimed he was going to his sister, Erna Bogopolsky, living at 251 W 93rd st, and the other, two weeks later, for Lotte Aberbach (arr 4 August 1939),[8] who stated she was going to her brother-in-law, Simon Bogopolsky at the same address. Julian named his mother-in-law, Erna Deutschmann, Isestrasse 74, Hamburg, as his nearest relative in Europe and Lotte named the same person at that same address as her mother.

Julian Aberbach appeared to be the brother of Erna Bogopolsky, suggesting that the Aberbach name, not Aberbaum, was meant for Erna's mothr.. The New York address of Simon and Erna clearly identify these two as living together as husband and wife, as they were declared such on their own passenger list with their two children and in their 1940 census entry.[9] Though we don't know the whole situation, a tentative conclusion can be made that Erna's maiden name is Erna Aberbach, and that she is the daughter of Helene Aberbach. It could be that Helene married twice or more, having children by several husbands.

Additional notes

To justify this conclusion, we must identify Helene Aberbach. To do this, we need more evidence.

Seven children were born to Mendel and Rifka (Vorlerer) Laxer in Berlin:[10] Esther, born 3 October 1876; Adolf, born 12 September 1878; an un-named child, born 1 July 1880; David, born 11 January 1883; Helene, born 13 January 1885; Salomon Israel, born 21 January 1887; and Else, born 20 February 1890. Of these seven children, three died very young.[11]

Mendel and the four remaining children (Esther, 16; Isaac, 12; Helene, 7; and Salomon Israel, 5) emigrated to Whitechapel, London, and on 2 May 1892, he and the

---

[7]   *New York, Passenger Lists, 1820-1957* (Ancestry.com), Year: 1939; Arrival: New York, New York; Microfilm Serial: T715, 1897-1957; Microfilm Roll: Roll 6367; Line: 3; Page Number: 129.

[8]   *New York, Passenger Lists, 1820-1957* (Ancestry.com), Year: 1939; Arrival: New York, New York; Microfilm Serial: T715, 1897-1957; Microfilm Roll: Roll 6375; Line: 1; Page Number: 134.

[9]   *Op. cit.*

[10]   *Berlin, Deutschland, Geburtsregister, 1874-1899* (Ancestry.com.de), for example, Helene Laxer, geboren 13. January 1885, Berlin, Berlin, Deutschland, Mutter: Rifka Laxer, Urkunde Nummer: 108, Laufendenummer: 723.

[11]   Adolf (tod 13 July 1879), David (tod 23 May 1884), and Else (tod 22 February 1890). Rifka may have died in cildbirth.

children were naturalized as British citizens.[12] Isaac, who was not named in the births registered in Berlin, being age 12 in 1892, was most likely the child born 1 July 1880. There is no evidence of Rifka in London so it is possible she died before the family left Germany.

Following naturalization, Esther Laxer[13] married Stanislaus Janklowicz Jan-Mar 1895 in Whitechapel.[14] Estera Janklowicz and Stanslaus returned to Germany, were arrested, and were deported to Terezin ghetto on 4 October 1942 where they perished.[15]

Helene married Max Aberbach Jan-Mar, 1905, also in Whitechapel.[16] Erna [Bogopolsky] was born[17] circa 1907 in Hamburg, the port of departure for her and Simon in 1938, and that her mother is Helene Aberbach, married in 1905 in Whitechapel, there is ample circumstantial evidence to suggest that Erna is the daughter of Max Aberbach and Helene Laxer. Such exquisite timing shows that Max and Helene must have gone to Hamburg from England almost directly after marriage.[18] Later, Helene had her German citizenship summarily annulled[19] and both Max and Helene were arrested by Nazi officials, deported to Auschwitz, and murdered, probably on 12 July 1942.[20]

We conclude at this point that Erna's maiden name is Aberbach but the question of Julian and Joachim still remains. How are these two really related to Erna? Can they claim to be her brothers? Does this affect the maiden name of Erna's mother?

Julian Aberbach was born 8 February 1909 in Vienna, Austria[21] and died 17 May

---

[12]   *Großbritannien, Einbürgerungszertifikate und -erklärungen, 1870-1912* (Ancestry). Mendel Lakser, male, age 38, b Jassy, Romania, certificate of naturalization for self, 2 May 1892, Whitechapel, Middlesex, England, father Barnett Lakser, mother Amelia Lakser, children: Esther Lakser, 16, Isaac Lakser, 12, Helena Lakser, 7, and Solomon Israel Lakser, 5. Image 769 of 1628. Piece 019, certificate numbers A6901-A7300.

[13]   Also spelled Lakser.

[14]   **http://www.findmypast.com/** *England & Wales marriages 1837-2008*. Esther Lakser, marr Stanislaus Yanklowitz, Whitechapel, London, England, Vol 1C, p 330.

[15]   **http://www.yadvashem.org/** "Estera Janklowicz nee Lakser was born in Berlin, Germany 3 October 1876. She was a housewife and married to Stanislaus. Prior to WWII she lived in Berlin, Germany. During the war she was in Berlin, Germany. Estera was murdered in the Shoah. This information is based on a Page of Testimony, no. 229, submitted by her nephew, Harold Janklowicz."

[16]   **http://www.findmypast.com/** *England & Wales marriages 1837-2008*. Helene Lakser, marr Max Aberbach (or Jacob Levy), Jan-Mar 1905, Whitechapel, London, England, Vol 1C, p 299. Max Aberbach, marr Helene Lakser (or Rachel Bitton), Jan-Mar 1905, Whitechapel, London, England, Vol 1C, p 299.

[17]   *New York, Passenger Lists, 1820-1957* (Ancestry). Year: 1938; Arrival: New York, New York; Microfilm Serial: T715, 1897-1957; Microfilm Roll: Roll 6267; Line: 6; Page Number: 159

[18]   Note: The address for Max Aberbach in Hamburg according to his telephone book entries (1928-1938) is Isestrasse 43. **http://www.ancestry.com.de/** *Deutsche Telefonbücher, 1915-1981.*

[19]   *Germany, Index of Jews Whose German Nationality was Annulled by Nazi Regime, 1935-1944* (Ancestry.com).

[20]   **http://www.yadvashem.org/** "Helena Aberbach, b 1885, was in Lodz, Poland, during the war. She was deported with transport T9, destination unknown. *Lodz Names - List of the ghetto inhabitants 1940-1944*, Yad V'ashem and the Organization of former residents of Lodz in Israel: Jerusalem, 1994." "Max Aberbach was born in Poland. He was married to Helen. Prior to WWII he lived in Berlin, Germany. Max was murdered in the Shoah. This information is based on a Page of Testimony, no. 251, submitted by his relative Frida Lowenhek."

[21]   *South Carolina, Naturalization Records, 1868-1991.* (Ancestry.com)

2004, Southampton, Suffolk, New York.[22] Joachim was born 8 August 1910, Voslau, Austria, and died 24 May 1992, Suffolk, New York.[23] Julian is not living with his wife, Lotte Aberbach, at the time of the 1940 census, but with his brother, Joachim;[24] Lotte had gone to California, applying for citizenship in Los Angeles.[25] Two years later, she was included in the city directory for Bisbee, Arizona,[26] and on 10 June 1950 married John Edward Bowman Merriman, as his second wife,[27] in Ventura county, California.[28] She died in Santa Barbara, 18 June 1971.[29]

Joachim arrived in the United States before his brother. He came as a single student in 1928.[30] If Julian and Joachim Aberbach are Erna's brothers, then his parents should be the same as hers, Max and Helene (Laxer) Aberbach. Their declared father,[31] Adolf Aberbach,[32] born 25 December 1878, Bolechow, Poland,[33] married Anna Jattir (or Schmetterling). She

---

[22]   *U.S. Social Security Death Index, 1935-2014.* (Ancestry.com)

[23]   *New York, Naturalization Records, 1882-1944* The National Archives and Records Administration; Washington. D. C.; Petitions for Naturalization from the U.S. District Court for the Southern District of New York, 1897-1944; Series: M1972; Roll: 1341. Joachim Aberbach (Jean De La Roche), b 12 Aug 1910, Austria, arr 1936, Petition for Naturalization, New York, USA, Southern District Court, New York, spouse Zita Aberbach. (Ancestry.com)

[24]   Joachim Aberbach household, *1940 federal census*, T627, Roll 2637, p 5314, ED 31-586, sheet 8A, lines 27-28, 240 W 73d St, New York, New York, New York, enumerated April 1940 by Janet Sagorin, family 15. (Ancestry.com)

[25]   *U.S. Naturalization Record Indexes, 1791-1992 (Indexed in World Archives Project)* (Ancestry.com). Lotte Aberbach, court California district, 4 April 1940, declaration 110509.

[26]   *U.S. City Directories, 1822-1995* (Ancestry.com). Mrs Lotte Aberbach, female, 510A Cole av, PO, Bisbee, Arizona, 1942.

[27]   John was born 28 December 1906, Riverside (*California Birth Index, 1905-1995* (Ancestry.com) and married Elizabeth Blanchard Kelsey 29 May 1929, Santa Paula, Ventura, California (*Marriage License and Certificate*). She was born 27 November 1906 in Los Angeles and married again before her death in 1997 (Elizabeth B. Howie, *U.S., Social Security Death Index, 1935-2014*). John died on his birthday in 1985, Ventura county (*U.S., Social Security Death Index, 1935-2014*).

[28]   *California, Marriage Index, 1949-1959* (Ancestry.com). John E Merriman, male, age 43, married Lottie Aberbach, aka Lottie Deutschmann, age 33 [sic], 10 June 1950, Ventura county, California.

[29]   *U.S., Social Security Death Index, 1935-2014* (Ancestry.com). Lottie Merriman, SSN 551-28-3998, last res 93105 Santa Barbara, Santa Barbara, California, b 11 October 1906, d June 1971, issued California bef 1951. *California, Death Index, 1940-1997* (Ancestry.com). Lottie Merriman, SSN 551-28-3998, b 11 October 1916, d 18 June 1971, Santa Barbara county.

[30]   *New York, Passenger Lists, 1820-1957,* (Ancestry.com), Year: 1928; Arrival: New York, New York; Microfilm Serial: T715, 1897-1957, Microfilm Roll: Roll 4265; Line: 10; Page Number: 219.

[31]   *New York, Passenger Lists, 1820-1957* (Ancestry.com), Year:1939; Arrival: New York, New York; Microfilm Serial: T715, 1897-1957; Microfilm Roll: Roll 6416; Line: 14; Page Number : 77, Julian named Adolf Aberbach as his father.

[32]   **https://www.familysearch.org/** Citing this Record: "Österreich, Niederösterreich, Wiener Meldezettel 1850-1896," database, FamilySearch (https://familysearch.org/ark:/61903/1:1:FR8L-266 : accessed 4 May 2016), Adolf Aberbach, 1908; citing Wien, Niederösterreich, Österreich, district II, Wiener Stadt- und Landesarchiv (Registration Office, Vienna City and Provincial Archives); FHL microfilm 1,277,215, Digital folder #004372082, image #00009.

[33]   *Galicia, Ukraine, Births, Marriages, and Deaths, 1789-1905* (Ancestry). Adolf Aberbach, birth 1878, Bolechow, L'viv, Ukraine. *California, Death Index,1940-1997* (Ancestry). Adolf Aberbach, male, b 25 December

was born 17 February 1883, Hamburg.[34] Adolf and Anna were passengers on the ill-fated *St. Louis* refugee ship which embarked from Hamburg 13 May 1939.[35] On 8 April 1940, Adolf arrived at New York with his wife, Anna.[36] In their passenger list, Adolf named Joachim Aberbach as "son," as did Anna. That year they lived at the same address as their sons but in a different apartment.[37]

So there is a confusion about the precise relationship between Julian and Erna (Aberbach) Bogopolsky. Are they really siblings? Or, did Julian claim to be her brother for some other reason?

Because of the timing of the futile cruise of the *St. Louis* from Hamburg to Havana and return, and Adolf's later arrival in New York, there appears to be only one Adolf-Anna couple. Still, there seems to be no family reason for Julian to claim Erna as his sister. As a guess, his claim may have been expedient for him to get on shore in New York. Certainly the current address of the Bogopolsky family was known to Julian as he arrived at New York, suggesting communication between the two families. The birth dates of Erna, Julian, and Joachim may indicate a childhood relationship among the three. Julian[38] Aberbach's mother-in-law and Erna's parents were close neighbors in Hamburg (living about 800 feet from one another).[39] Or, the declaration may simply have been in error.

Another possibility for Julian's claim lies in the terrible situation Jewish people were facing at this critical time. This possibility is represented in the reported comments by Jesus Christ while he was in the process of being crucified. As he looked down from the cross to the assembled on-lookers, he addressed his mother, referring to his disciple, John, "Woman, behold thy son!" and to John, "Behold thy mother!"[40] He was giving John the responsibility

---

1878, d 2 April 1959, Los Angeles county, mother's maiden name Rosenman. *JewishGen Online Worldwide Burial Registry (JOWBR)* (Ancestry). Adolf Aberbach, hebrew name Aharon ben Yoel David, b 25 December 1878, d 2 April 1959, buried Sag Harbor, New York, cemetery ID USA-01754, spouse Anna, *U.S., Social Security Applications and Claims Index, 1936-2007* (Ancestry). Adolf Aberbach, SSN 555-42-4893, b 25 December 1878.

[34] Citing this Record: *Österreich, Niederösterreich, Wiener Meldezettel 1850-1896*, database, FamilySearch (**https://familysearch.org/ark:/61903/1:1:FR8L-266** : accessed 4 May 2016), The maiden name (Schmetterling) for Anna is supplied in a Virginia marriage record for her son Joachim Aberbach. *Virginia, Marriage Records, 1936-2014* (Ancestry). Certificate of Marriage, Commonwealth of Virginia, #13190, Joachim Jean Aberbach and Susan Tema (Clumpus) Hamburger, Arlington, Virginia, 15 May 1964.

[35] *The St Louis Passengers*, a listing available on Yad V'ashem.org. "Partial list of passengers of the ship *St Louis*, that embarked from Hamburg on 13/05/1939."

[36] *New York, Passenger Lists, 1820-1957* (Ancestry). Year: 1940; Arrival: New York, New York; Microfilm Serial: T715, 1897-1957; Microfilm Roll: Roll 6457; Line: 1; Page Number: 30.

[37] Adolph Aberbach household, *1940 federal census*, T627, Roll 2637, p 5316, ED 31-586, sheet 10A, lines 33-34, 240 W 73d St, New York, New York, New York, enumerated April 1940 by Janet Sagarin, family 111. (Ancestry.com)

[38] Just to tie up loose ends, Joachim Jean Aberbach used an alias of Jean de la Roche and traveled extensively alone and with his wife, Zita. He divorced Zita and married Susan Tema (Clumpus) Hamburger in Virginia. He was b 12 August 1910, Vöslau, Austria, and died 24 May 1992, Suffolk, New York. Julian Jackson Aberbach, was b 8 February 1909, Vienna, Austria, and died 17 May 2004, Southampton, Suffolk, New York. Julian owned the rights to the recordings of Elvis Presley!

[39] Based on current conditions via Google Maps.

[40] John 19: 26-27.

of caring for his mother as her oldest child. Jesus was acting as a Jew, as he did all his life, following typical Jewish social customs.

In this present situation, the Aberbach parents, Adolf and Anna, narrowly escaping almost certain death by being allowed to leave the *St. Louis* to go to England instead of remaining in Europe. About half of the passengers who went to Holland, Belgium, or France were rounded up and murdered once Nazi troops had overwhelmed those countries. Of those who went to England, all but one person survived. Knowing that Erna's parents were living in Hamburg, the Aberbachs may have felt a responsibility for her and by this means stated publicly that Erna was considered , by them, to be "one of the family."

Conclusion

Based on our knowledge of Erna's parents in Hamburg, and the Adolf Aberbach family, also of Hamburg, it appears clear that Erna's declaration of the name of her mother is a true statement. Regardless of Julian's claim to be Erna's brother, there is high confidence in saying that we now know Erna's maiden name.

Chapter 4

The Birth Family of Amelia (Alpiger) Lentz[1]

Introduction

Research always has its interesting turns and twists. Sometimes, a brick wall arises simply because of the order of the discoveries. A page in a document is turned and a serendipitous entry appears leading down a path – which dead-ends. So, back to the point of departure and choose a new path. Even with the best practices, every research problem has its surprises.

In the present case, working in the normal way from what is known to what is unknown an ancestor appeared whose family immigrated to the United States from Switzerland and settled in Louisville, Kentucky. Her name is Amelia (Alpiger) Lentz.[2] She appeared as the wife of William Lentz, the mother of many children but none of her children seemed to know much about her. Her parents are not named in her death certificate, even though the informant is Louis C. Lentz, Amelia's son.[3]

It is not unusual for children to be ignorant of the background of their parents so that when they are called upon to be the informant for a death record or the census, inaccuracies and blanks or the well-worn phrase "don't know" are among the results. So the question remains, who is her family?

Amelia and her siblings

Amelia Alpiger was born April 1859 in Switzerland.[4] She came to the US, age 19, with her siblings[5] and settled with them in Louisville, Ky, where she married William Lentz,

---

[1]   Permission to use this problem was given by Roni Stern, 3 April 2017.

[2]   Also known as Emily, Emma, Emmy, or Emelia (Alpiger) Lentz.

[3]   *Kentucky, Death Records, 1852-1964*, (Ancestry). Certificate, reg dist 755, prime reg dist 2275, file#16584, reg# 2844, 168 N William, Louisville, Jefferson, Ky, Amelia Lentz, female, white, married, d 10 June 1936.

[4]   William Lentz household, *1900 federal census*, T623, Roll 533, p 16B, ED 144, sheet 16B, lines 54-63, Indian Hill Precinct, Magisterial Dist #1, Jefferson, Kentucky, enumerated 16 June 1900 by Conrad J Clausen, dwelling 270, family 282. (Ancestry).

[5]   *New York, Passenger Lists, 1820-1957* (Ancestry), arr 30 October 1878, dep Rotterdam, arr NY, NY, ship *P Caland*. Her siblings are named only with initials, age, and gender. (Ancestry).

c1879.[6] They had ten children over the next twenty years[7] and she died in 1936; her husband died in 1941,[8] both in Louisville. She did not appear with both parents in any census.

The Alpiger name is uncommon in the United States, especially at the early date when Amelia came to this country. To begin to unravel the problem, look for passenger arrival records for New York. There are only two early examples of the Alpiger name. The first is Carl Alpiger, age 46 (born c1825) who arrived 22 February 1871, alone, on the ship *Brooklyn*, from Liverpool.[9] This document raised a question because Carl Alpiger did not appear in any later public records. In 1880, Christ Alpiger, aged 55, lived alone, a widower and umbrella mender.[10] In 1900 Christian lived aged 75, born June 1824, with his wife, Catherine, born February 1844, and several children, including a step-daughter, Lena Hoefflin, born September 1879 in Kentucky, divorced, mother of two children, both dead.[11] In 1910 Christian appeared (age 85, married 3 times), with Catherine (married twice).[12] It seems reasonable that Christian was mistakenly entered as Carl in the 1871 passenger record.

As a side note, Lena Hoefflin had a son, Edwin/Edward W Hoefflin (born 23 July 1902, died 7 March 1939, Louisville),[13] and married a man named Charles Moeller.[14] At her

---

[6]   Christian Alpiger household, *1910 federal census*, T624, Roll 483, p 73A/B, ED 6, sheet 14A, lines 48-50, 51-55, Indian Hills, Jefferson, Kentucky, enumerated 4 May 1910 by C G Nathmiller, dwelling 266, family 273, married 29 years. (Ancestry). William Lentz household, *1930 federal census*, T626, Roll 752, p 16, ED 56-180, sheet 3A, lines 42-43, District 1, Jefferson, Kentucky, enumerated 4 April 1930 by Effie T Coburn, dwelling 68, family 71, age 20 at first marriage. (Ancestry)

[7]   William Lentz household, *1910 federal census*, T624, Roll 483, pp 73A/B, ED 6, sheets 14A/B, lines 48-50, 51-55, Indian Hills, Jefferson, Kentucky, enumerated 4 May 1910 by C G Mattmiller, dwelling 266, family 283. (Ancestry).

[8]   *Kentucky, Death Records, 1852-1964*, (Ancestry). Certificate, reg dist 755, prime reg dist 2275, file# 17345, reg# 3089, St Anthony's Hospital, Louisville, Jefferson, Ky, res 168 N William St, Louisville, Jefferson, Ky, William Lentz, d 15 July 1941.

[9]   *New York, Passenger Lists, 1820-1957* (Ancestry). Carl Alpiger, age 46 (b ca 1825), male, German, from Germany, arr 22 February 1871, dep Liverpool, England, arr NYC, ship *Brooklyn*. (Ancestry).

[10]   Christ Alpiger household, *1880 federal census*, T9, Roll 422, p 50A, ED 109, line 6, Louisville, Jefferson, Kentucky, enumerated 9 June 1880 by James M Hallnan, dwelling 298, family 530. (Ancestry). Living at 233 Clay st, Louisville.

[11]   Christian Alpiger household, *1900 federal census*, T623, Roll 529, p 283B, ED 40, sheet 1B, lines 60-65, 518 Jefferson St, ward 4, Louisville, Jefferson, Kentucky, enumerated 2 June 1900 by Edward D White, dwelling 6, family 15. (Ancestry).

[12]   Christian Alpiger household, *1910 federal census*, T624, Roll 484, p 45, ED 66, sheet 10A, lines 28-31, 619 East Walnut St, ward 3, Louisville, Jefferson, Kentucky, enumerated 22 April 1910 by Gil Potter Haynes, dwelling 147, family 260. (Ancestry).

[13]   *Kentucky, Death Records, 1852-1964* (Ancestry). Certificate #7367, for Edwin Hoeflin, married Clara Lammers, electrician, born Louisville, Kentucky. Father W C Hoeflin, mother Lena Alpiger.

[14]   Charles Mooeler household, *1920 federal census*, T625, Roll 578, p 213, ED 93, sheet 9A, lines 13-15, 532 Grey Street, ward 4, Louisville, Jefferson, Kentucky, enumerated 9 January 1920 by Charles G Frost, dwelling 151, family 227; Edward W Hoeffling household, *1930 federal census*, T624, Roll 756, p 116B, ED 56-87, sheet 9B, lines 70-74, 106 St Catherine St, Louisville, Jefferson, Kentucky, enumerated 8 April 1930 by Mrs Anna E Pemberton, dwelling 95, family 225; Clara Hoefflin household, *1940 federal census*, T627, Roll 1368, p 1283, ED 121-108A, sheet 61A, lines 20-25, 537 E Chestnut, Louisville, Jefferson, Kentucky, enumerated April 1940 by Howard Simms, family 7, rents home $14/mo. (Ancestry)

death in 1949, her unknown informant did not know the names of her parents.[15]

On 30 October 1878, a second Alpiger arrival in New York aboard the ship *P Caland*, showed: C Alpiger, female, age 42, occupation "none," and six individuals labeled as "family:" C Alpiger, female, age 23; C Alpiger, female, age 21, E Alpiger, female, age 19, B Alpiger, female, age 9, A Alpiger, male, age 8, and E Mehrling, female, age 9, all born Switzerland.[16] It is sensible to look for all Alpiger names in the 1880 census to get full names and ages. The 1880 census contained two Alpiger males living in Louisville. One is mentioned above, the second was a 4-year-old boy, Henry, a pupil at the German Orphan's Asylum on Jefferson street.[17]

The presence of Henry Alpiger brought a pause in the research to identify who he was and to whom he belonged. Kentucky mortuary records revealed two deaths early in 1878, before the Alpiger family arrival. One was a male child, Christ Alpiger, stillborn and buried on 24 April 1878[18] and the second was Christiana Alpiger, a 41-year old woman (born c1837), who died of a "difficult childbirth," on 2 May with burial two days later.[19] These two are probably a son and deceased wife of Christian.

The fact that Christiana was not on the 1871 passenger arrival record with Christian (Carl) and that 4-year old Henry was born in Kentucky, suggests that Christian Alpiger married Christiana after his arrival in Kentucky, and that she died after bearing two children, first Henry (1876), and second Christ (1878). This may account for the fact that Christian is listed as a widower in the 1880 census.

The Oct, 1878, arrival of five Alpiger "siblings" with an older Alpiger woman, born c1836, raises the possibility that Christian was also a widower (or divorced) when he entered the United States and that his children had been left behind in Switzerland, perhaps with their mother or some other relative. After a careful search, an Albitter family was found in the Louisville census for 1880, on "East Green st, north side." The head of household was Ebelina Albitter, age 44, civil condition not marked, midwife[20] with dropsy, and five of her children: Christian, male, age 24, single; Katherine, female, age 23, single; Emelia, female, age 21, married; Alfred, male, age 15, single; and Bertha, female, age 12, all born in Switzerland. As unlikely as it may sound, the claim that Ebelina is the mother of all five of

[15]   *Kentucky, Death Records, 1852-1964*, (Ancestry). Certificate # 23297, Lena Moeller Hoefflin, died 1 November 1949, Shively, Jefferson, Kentucky.
[16]   *New York, Passenger Lists, 1820-1957.* (Ancestry). One additional "family" member, E Mehrling, F, age 9, was missing from the 1880 listing for this group.
[17]   Henry Alpeger household, *1880 federal census*, T9, Roll 424, p 348C, ED 147, line 11, German Protestant Asylum, 758 Jefferson St, Louisville, Jefferson, Kentucky, enumerated 5 June 1880 by W E Brown, dwelling 236, family 247. (Ancestry).
[18]   [Kentucky] *Mortuary Record for April 1878*, #28, Christ Alpiger, male, white, stillborn, Dr Prim, 24th [Apr, 1878], City [Louisville, Ky], #345 East Jefferson, burial 24th [Apr 1878], Eastern Cemetery, undertaker Schaefer. (Ancestry).
[19]   [Kentucky] *Mortuary Record for May 1878*, #2, Christiana Alpiger, female, white, married, age 41, difficult labor, Drs [...]eeland & Prim, d May 2d [1878], b Germany, Jeff[erson st] bet[ween] Clay & Shelby, buried May 3d [1878], Eastern [Cemetery], undertaker Schaefer. (Ancestry).
[20]   Ebelina Albitter household, *1880 federal census*, T9, Roll 422, p 161B, ED 114, lines , 193 East Green, North Side, Louisville, Jefferson, Kentucky, enumerated 3 June 1880 by F F Dressen, dwelling , family 161. Ebelina's civil condition is not marked though Emelia is marked as married. (Ancestry).

the children strengthens the possibility that she is the ex-wife of Christian Alpiger, now come to Kentucky.

Comparing this group with the 1878 passenger list, there is one change of gender and one age difference but overall equivalence.

Comparison of the Alpiger children from three sources

1878 Passenger record	1880 "Albitter household"	Death notices/records
C, female, age 42 (b c1836)	Ebelina, female, age 44 (b c1836)	not found
C, female, age 21 (b c1856)	Christian, male, age 24 (b c1856)	Christian J, male, b 26 Feb 1855[21]
C, female, age 20 (b c1857)	Katherine, female, age 23 (b c1857)	not found
E, female, age 19 (b c1859)	Emilia, female, age 21 (b c1859)	Amelia, female, b May 1859[22]
A, male, age 8 (b c1870)	Alfred, male, age 15 (b c1865)	Alfred G, male, b 10 January 1865[23]
B, female, age 9 (b c1869)	Bertha, female, age 12 (b c1868)	Anna Bertha, female, b c1868[24]

The three marriages of Christian Alpiger

There are no known marriage records for the three marriages of Christian Alpiger though the approsimate dates for each can be estimated. Christian Alpiger certainly married his first wife before his first child was born in Switzerland in 1855. By the time he arrived in the United States in 1871, he was again single. He married his second wife, Christiana, before the birth of Henry in 1876, in Kentucky. Christiana died in 1878 and he was again single. He married his third wife, Katherine, about 1881 in Louisville.

Alfred Alpiger's parents are named as Christian Alpiger and Anna Katherine Eblin in his death record. The Eblin name also shows up in Alfred's son, Eblin W Alpiger.[25] Christian J Alpiger's parents are named as Christian Alpiger and Marie Eblin, both born Switzerland. Anna Bertha Gee's parents are given only as Alpiger and Anna on her death record.[26] Based on this evidence, Christian's first wife was named Marie or Anna Katherine

---

[21] *Kentucky, Death Records, 1852-1964*, (Ancestry). Certificate, reg dist <blank>, prime reg dist 2275, file# 15252, reg# 2238, Lampton Cranne & Ramey Co, 15th by the sta[tion], Louisville, Jefferson, Ky, Christian J Alpiger, male, white, widowed, d 28 July 1921, b 26 February 1855, age 66y 5m 2d packer for Lampton Crane & Ramey Co, b Switzerland, father Christian Alpiger, b Switzerland, mother Marie Eblin, b Switzerland, informant Otto C Alpiger, Louisville, Ky.

[22] *Kentucky, Death Records, 1852-1964*, (Ancestry). Certificate, reg dist 755, prime reg dist 2275, file#16584, reg# 2844, 168 N William, Louisville, Jefferson, Ky, Amelia Lentz, female, white, married, d 10 June 1936, husband William Lentz, b May 1859, age 77y 1m ?d, housewife, b Switzerland, father don't know, b don't know, mother don't know, b don't know, informant Louis C Lentz.

[23] *Kentucky, Death Records, 1852-1964*, (Ancestry). Certificate, reg dist 755, prime reg dist 2275, file# 15434, reg# 3294, 917 Schiller, Louisville, Jefferson, Ky, res 917 Schiller, Louisville, Jefferson, Ky, Alfred G Alpiger, d 19 July 1946, male, white, widower, wife Carrie Alpiger, b 10 January 1865, age 81y 6m 9d, b Switzerland.

[24] Frederick Gee household, *1930 federal census*, T626, Roll 762, p 176, ED 23, sheet 12A, lines 33-35, 2206 Center, Covington, Kenton, Kentucky, enumerated 17 April 1930 by John F Eifert, jr, dwelling 221, family 253. (Ancestry). *The Cincinnatti Enquirer*, Friday, 19 March 1943, p 17, column 3. "Mrs Anna B Gee." (Newspapers.com)

[25] Alfred G. Alpiger household, *1900 federal census*, T623, Roll 529, p 172B, ED 34, sheet 6B, lines 82-88, 626 Breckinridge St, ward 3, Louisville, Jefferson, Kentucky, enumerated 5 June 1900 by Theodore R Ctierle, dwelling 104, family 135. (Ancestry). Eblin was born November 1894.

[26] *Ohio Deaths, 1908-1953*, Certificate 16984, 17 March 1943, Cincinnati, Hamilton, Ohio. Father is "Alpiger" and mother "Anna" both born Switzerland. FamilySearch.org.

Eblin (also known as Ebelina).

The two children of Christiana, born in Louisville were, first, Henry Nickel Alpiger, born 17 July 1876,[27] d 11 June 1950, Louisville.[28] His parents were not identified in his death record. The second child, Christ, was probably responsible for Christiana's death. There is no direct evidence about Christiana's maiden name but the mother's maiden name is often memorialized by using it as a name for one or more children. It shouldn't surprise anyone that Christiana's maiden name could be Nicoll, Nicol, Nickle, Nichol, Nicholl, or some variant.[29]

Mary M (Alpiger) Ditsch was born April 1882, Louisville, died 19 January 1956, Louisville.[30] Her parents are identified in her death record as Chris Alpiger and Kathrine Nicoll. Also, a second child, Elizabeth Agnes (Alpiger) Duncan, born 11 August 1885, Louisville,[31] married Harry R Duncan[32] but was separated from him before his death[33] and reclaimed her maiden name.[34]

Because the informant for Mary Ditsch's death certificate was the records department of the hospital in which she died, their declaration of her parents' names may not carry as much weight as the considerations given above for the maiden name of Christiana, mother of Henry Alpiger. Even so, there remains some uncertainty about the maiden names of these two women though for this problem the name Nicholl is given to Christiana.

Discussion

Alpiger entries in the Louisville City Directories begin with Christian alone in 1877, 1878, and 1879.[35] Then, in 1880 and 1881, appeared Catherine Alpiger, widow [of]

---

[27]   *WWI Draft Registration Cards 1917-1918* (Ancestry). Roll 1653505, bd 2, Henry Nickel Alpiger, 8246 Washington, Louisville, Ky, age 42, b 17 July 1876, white, native born citizen, works at soft drink stand for self, 300 E Market, Louisville, Ky, nearest relative Annie Alpiger,

[28]   *Kentucky, Death Records, 1852-1964*, (Ancestry). Certificate, reg dist 755, prime reg dist 2275, file# 50-16295, reg#2747, Baptist Hospital, Louisville, Jefferson, Ky, 1839 Alfresco Place, Louisville, Jefferson, Ky, Henry N Alpiger, d 11 June 1950, male, white, widowed, b 17 July 1876, age 73y, retired cafe owner, b Louisville, Ky, father and mother unknown, informant Miss Henrietta Alpiger.

[29]   The surname Alpiger and Eblin, are found in the Zurich region of Switzerland. *Register of Swiss Surnames, Polygraphischer Verlag, Zürich 1989.* **http://www.genealogy.net/reg/CH/famnam-m.htm.** Alpiger (Cantons: Appenzell-Outer Rhodes, Teufen and St Gall, Alt St Johann, Gams, and Wildhaus); Eblin (Canton Grisons, Chur). This web site is outdated now: **http://wiki-de.genealogy.net/Hauptseite**.

[30]   *Kentucky, Death Records, 1852-1964*, (Ancestry). Certificate 116-56-1150, reg dist 755, prime reg dist 6101, reg #312, died at Central State Hospital, Lakeland, Jefferson, Ky, res 1839 Alfresco, Louisville, Jeff, Ky, Mary Ditsch, d 19 January 1956, female, white, married, b 24 August 1882, age 73yrs, housewife, b Kentucky, father Chris Alpiger, mother Kathrine Nicoll, informant Record-Central State Hospital.

[31]   *Kentucky Births and Christenings, 1839-1960*, database, FamilySearch (**https://familysearch.org/ark:/61903/1:1:FWNX-1VT** : 4 December 2014), Elisabeth Alpiger, 11 August 1885; citing St. Paul's Evangelical, Louisville, Jefferson, Kentucky; FHL microfilm 1,531,413.

[32]   *Kentucky, Marriage Records, 1852-1914.* (Ancestry).

[33]   *Kentucky, Death Records, 1852-1964*, (Ancestry). Certificate, reg dist 755, prime reg dist 2275, file# 12578, reg# 2881

[34]   Theodore Rosenbaum household, *1940 federal census*, T627, Roll 1365, p 185, ED 121-17, sheet 5A, lines 24-30, 133 Stevenson, Louisville, Jefferson, Kentucky, enumerated 5 April 1940 by Jean Louise Long, family 106. (Ancestry)

[35]   *Caron's Directory of the City of Louisville, for 1877*, [Louisville, Ky]: C. K. Caron, 1877. Ancestry. Also 1878 and 1879. (Ancestry).

Christian,[36] as well as Christian (jr) in 1880, Alfred,[37] in 1881, and later, Bertha[38] and Henry.[39]

The only confusing entry in these directories is the one for Catherine, who is not likely to be young Katherine Albitter (b 1857), daughter of Ebelina Albitter. Remember that both Alfred and Christian were the declared sons of Christian and Anna Katherine (or Marie) Eblin. The 1880 city directory listing for Catherine Alpiger (widow Christian) showed a residence address of 14 Baxter av, nr Jefferson, which was also the boarding address of Christian Alpiger (teacher).[40] The census for that year also showed that Ebelina and Christian are mother and son. Thus, Catherine is Ebelina Albitter also known as Anna Katherine (Eblin) Alpiger, the mother of Christian, jr, and his siblings, including Amelia. These facts identify the parents of Amelia.

Clearly, unless Christian's marriage with Christiana was bigamous, he must have divorced Anna Katherine prior to leaving Switzerland, perhaps subsequently helping her to bring their children to America in 1878. It is not uncommon for divorced (or abandoned) women of this time to claim widowhood (see the case of Emeline and Mitch Evins in Chapter 10). Catherine disappeared from the directory in 1881 suggesting that she finally succumbed to dropsy.[41]

Because Henry Nickle Alpiger was born in Louisville in 1876 and Christ in 1878, probable son of Christiana, who died in childbirth and because Christian (b 1825) was a widower in 1880, it is very likely that Christian and his second wife, Christiana, are the parents of Henry[42] and Christ.

His third and final wife was Katherine (---) Hoeflin, see the Timeline, below.

---

[36]   *Caron's Directory of the City of Louisville, for 1880*, [Louisville, Ky]: C. K. Caron, 1880. (Ancestry). Also 1881.

[37]   *Caron's Directory of the City of Louisville, for 1881*, [Louisville, Ky]: C. K. Caron, 1881. (Ancestry). Also 1888.

[38]   *Caron's Directory of the City of Louisville, for 1886*, [Louisville, Ky]: C. K. Caron, 1886. (Ancestry). Also 1888, 1890, and 1891.

[39]   *Caron's Directory of the City of Louisville, for 1894*, [Louisville, Ky]: C. K. Caron, 1894. (Ancestry).

[40]   *Caron's Directory of the City of Louisville, for 1880*, [Louisville, Ky]: C. K. Caron, 1880. (Ancestry).

[41]   Dropsy is a condition now known as edema which is a deteriorating circulatory problem resulting in the collection of fluid underneath the skin and in body cavities. Because this condition may indicate a heart abnormality dropsy was usually considered a serious problem, one which could easily be fatal.

[42]   *Louisville Courier Journal* for Friday, 12 June 1936, p 41, col 7, states: "Lentz, - Wednesday,June 10, 1936, at 5 am, Amelia Lentz, age 77 years, beloved wife of William Lentz, mother of Louis C, Charles F, Frank A, Clarence X, and Otto W Lentz, Mrs Minnie Miller, Mrs Virginia Sillman, Mrs Lillian Holderer, and Mrs Anna Kamber, and sister of Alfred and *Henry Alpiger* and Mrs Bertha Gee. ... Interment in Cave Hill Cemetery." (Newspapers.com)

Timeline for Christian Alpiger (1824-1911),
his three wives and nine children:

Date	Event	Place
1824, 4 Jun	Birth of Christian Alpiger	Switzerland
c1836	Birth of Ebelina Albitter (Anna Katherine or Marie Eblin)	Switzerland
c1837	Birth of Christiana (Nicholl)	- - -
1845, 28 Feb	Birth of Katherine (- - -)	Germany
	Marriage No. 1 begins	
c1853	Marr of Christian Alpiger & Anna Katherine (or Marie) Eblin	Switzerland
1855, 26 Feb	Birth of first child, Christian J Alpiger	Switzerland
c1857	Birth of second child, Katherine Alpiger	Switzerland
1859, Apr	Birth of third child, Amelia (Alpiger) Lentz	Switzerland
1865, 10 Jan	Birth of fourth child Alfred G Alpiger	Switzerland
c1868	Birth of fifth child, Anna Bertha (Alpiger) Gee	Switzerland
c1868-71	Suspected divorce of Christian Alpiger and Katherine Eblin	Switzerland
	Marriage No. 1 ends (divorce)	
1871, 22 Feb	Arrival of Carl (Christian) Alpiger	New York City
c1874-5	Marriage of Christian Alpiger & Christiana (Nicholl)	Louisville
	Marriage No. 2 begins	
1876, 17 Jul	Birth of sixth child, Henry Nickel Alpiger	Louisville
1878, 24 Apr	Stillbirth, burial of seventh child, Christ Alpiger, East Cemetery	Louisville
1878, 2 May	Death of Christiana (Nicholl) Alpiger	Louisville
1878, 4 May	Burial of Christiana (Nicholl) Alpiger, East Cemetery	Louisville
	Marriage No. 2 ends (death)	
1878, 30 Oct	Arrival of C Alpiger and 5 children (family)	New York City
1879, Sep	Birth of step-daughter Lena Hoefflin	Louisville
c1880	Death of Mr Hoefflin	Louisville
1880, 1 Jun	Census, Christian Alpiger, widow	Louisville
1880, 1 Jun	Census, Henry Alpiger, age 4, German Orphan's Asylum	Louisville
1880, 1 Jun	Census, Ebelina Albitter and 5 children	Louisville
c1881	Possible death of Ebelina Albitter ("widow of Christian")	Louisville
c1880-1	Marriage of Christian Alpiger & Katherine (- - -) Hoefflin	Louisville
	Marriage No. 3 begins	
1882, 24 Aug	Birth of eighth child, Mary M (Alpiger) Ditsch	Louisville
1885, Aug	Birth of ninth child, Elizabeth Agnes (Alpiger) Duncan	Louisville
1900, 1 Jun	Census, Christian & Catherine Alpiger (marr 19 years)	Louisville
1910, 15 Apr	Census, Christian (m 3x) & Catherine (m 2x) Alpiger (m 29y)	Louisville
1911, 13 Feb	Death of Christian Alpiger	Louisville
1911, 15 Feb	Burial of Christian Alpiger, Cave Hill Cemetery	Louisville
	Marriage No. 3 ends (death)	
1919, 11 Oct	Death of Katherine ((- - -), Hoefflin) Alpiger	Louisville
1919, 13 Oct	Burial of Katherine ((- - -), Hoefflin) Alpiger, Cave Hill Cem	Louisville
1936, 10 Jun	Death of Amelia (Alpiger) Lentz	Louisville
1936, 12 Jun	Burial of Amelia (Alpiger) Lentz, Cave Hill Cemetery	Louisville

Chapter 5

Widows, Stepkin, and Support Networks:
Clues to the Unknown Father of Miranda (Taylor) Morris[1]

> Traditional literature favors accounts of families split asunder by remarriages and incompatible steprelationships. Less publicized are the marital kinships that strengthened families, extended them, and – consequently – expanded the options that genealogists must consider. Miranda (Taylor) Morris makes this point.

Birth identities for married females of past centuries are notoriously difficult to establish. If lucky, a researcher will find the woman's marriage record, whereon some surname is given – usually with no indication as to whether it is a maiden name or a prior husband's name. For that record to identify parents also is almost beyond hope. If truly lucky, a researcher may find that the region's records have been well abstracted, indexed, and published; and that one or another index links the bride to a parental will or deed of gift. But seldom is this the reality a genealogist faces when tracking a fmaily across America's frontier. Instead, one often must labor to build a case for the woman's birth family – by studying the males to whom she was attached, by studying the entire pool of males within her area who bore her birth surname, by expanding the research to include stepkin, and by following all those males whenever and wherever the itch to move may have led them.

The point is made often in today's methodological lectures on the subject of tracking ancestral females.[2] It still is often ignored. Miranda (Taylor) Morris proves both the validity of the advice and the extent of the labor it entails.

Miranda and her children

The Widow Morris died in 1876.[3] In her forty-nine years, she had trekked across some three thousand miles of the American frontier. Like most pioneers of her era, she migrated in stages – at least four of them. From her native Virginia, she crossed the rugged

---

[1]   "Widows, Stepkin and Support Networks: Clues to the Unknown Father of Miranda (Taylor) Morris," *National Genealogical Society Quarterly*, Vol 84, #1, March 1996, pp 17-28.

[2]   For example, see Elizabeth Shown Mills, "Finding Females: Name Unknown, Parents Unknown, Origins Unknown," National Genealogical Society's 1991 Conference in the States, Portland; available from Repeat Performance; 2911 Crabapple Lane; Hobart, IN 46342.

[3]   *Saline County (Kansas) Journal*, 26 April 1876, p. 3, col. 1.

Appalachians and the Mississippi to settle in Warren County, Missouri (or perhaps in Montgomery County, from which Warren was cut in 1833). There, she married Nathaniel Morris on 28 August 1847,[4] before a Baptist minister named Thomas Bowen. Over the next fifteen years, Miranda bore seven children, all in Missouri – John (1847-8), William (1849-50), Mary E. (1852), Charles (1854), Martha (1856), Louella (1859-60), and Eli A. (1861-2).[5]

By 1870, Miranda was again a feme sole, still landless like many postwar widows, eking out an existence for herself and children. But they were not in Missouri. They had ascended the Mississippi nearly a thousand miles, into Grant County, Wisconsin.[6] Miranda would make two more moves in the next five years – following her son William's new in-laws westward into Iowa, then onto the plains of Kansas, where she apparently homesteaded. The agricultural schedule of the 1875 state census of Kansas's Rice County credits her with 160 unfenced acres worth $300. Four of those acres were planted in corn. She and the two children still at home were the owners of one cow and one dog.[7] It is doubtful they had accumulated much more before consumption felled her the next spring, 10 April 1876.[8]

True to the life of most females of her era, Miranda created few records of her own. The counties in which she lived offer no probate, church, or court records to document her identity, much less her trials. Yet indirect pointers to her kinsmen can be found by closely analyzing the few records of her husband and by studying their details in conjunction with the larger body of records existing for contemporaries of her surname and the families into which these intermarried.

Her husband

Nathaniel Morris was also born in Virginia, about 1819-21.[9] The 1850 and 1860 censuses of Warren County call him a "farmer;" but, like many other husbandmen of his era, he showed little interest in landownership. Small-scale farming could be done on rental parcels or unclaimed public land. Thus, Nathaniel created few records at the Warren County courthouse. One small tract of 40 acres that he purchased in 1855 was sold just a few days later, at nearly double the price – an aberrant transaction for him. The plot's legal description – i.e., northeast quarter of southwest quarter of section 5, township 47 north, range 2 west

---

[4]   Warren Co., Mo., Marriage Book B: 150; see also Mrs. Howard W. Woodruff, *The Marriage Records of Warren County, Missouri, Books "A" and "B," 1833-1860* (Kansas City, Mo.: Privately printed, 1969), 23.

[5]   1850 U.S. census, population schedule, Warren Co., Mo., 99th district, p. 74, dwelling 705, family 705; 1860 U.S. Cens., pop. sch., Warren Co., Campbranch township, Pin Oak post office, p. 186, dwell. 394, fam. 395; 1870 U.S. Cens., pop. sch.,, Grant Co., Wis., Potosi twp., Plattesville, p.o., p. 3, dwell. 18, fam. 18; 1875 Kans. State cens., Rice Co., Farmer twp., Atlanta p.o., dwell. 91, fam. 91. The pop. sch. Of this state cens., which says that she last lived in Iowa, erroneously gives Miranda's name as *Margaret*; the agricultural sch. cites it as *Myranda*.

[6]   1870 U.S. Cens., pop. sch., Grant Co., Wis., Potosi twp., Plattesville p.o., p. 3, dwell. 18, fam. 18.

[7]   1875 Kans. state cens., agr. sch. Rice Co., Farmer twp., Atlanta p.o. The family with which she moved from Wis. To Iowa to Kans. Was the Bonhams. See family record of Edmund James Bonham, Los Angeles, Calif., dated 1920; unpublished manuscript in possession of the present writer. Edmund James was the brother of Anna Eliza Bonham, who married William Eleazar Morris.

[8]   *Saline County (Kansas) Journal*, 26 April 1876, p. 3, col. 1.

[9]   1850 U.S. Census, population schedule, Warren Co., Mo., 99th district, p. 74, dwelling 705, family 705; 1860 U.S. Cens., pop. sch., Warren Co., Campbranch township, Pin Oak post office, p. 186, dwell. 394, fam. 395;

– could be immensely important.[10] When platted on a county map, the land falls just northwest of the county seat of Warrenton. See figure 1.

Nathaniel made no other court appearances in Warren. No military service can be established for him. The timing of his last child, circa 1861-62, suggests that he may not have lived through the Civil War; but no Union or Confederate records of Missouri's sorely divided population seem to relate to this Nathaniel Morris.[11] Whether he moved with Miranda and children to Wisconsin is unknown. No probate record has been found in either locale – a not surprising fact, because he apparently died without real estate or chattel of significant value.

Assessing the problem

Sometime between Eli's birth in 1861-62 and the date of the 1870 census data, Miranda lost her husband. Sometime during that block of years, she and the children (with or without Nathaniel) relocated in Wisconsin. These facts raise several questions about Miranda which, if they can be answered, might lead to the identification of her parents.

> o How did Miranda, who was born in Virginia, come to be in Warren County, Missouri in 1847, aged nineteen to twenty-one?
> o Why did Miranda leave Missouri after 1861-62?
> o Why did she choose to relocate in Grant County, Wisconsin?

Given Miranda's youth at her first appearance in Missouri, it is reasonable to conclude that she likely migrated there with her family. As a working hypothesis, it is reasonable to begin with the premise that her family's surname was the one under which she married: Taylor.

Identifying a pool of candidates

To test the hypothesis, all contemporary households of the Taylor surname in Warren County, Missouri, were identified and studied. That exercise yielded nine possibilities – two appearing in 1835-40 probate records and seven more appearing on the 1840 census.

---

[10]   Warren Co., Deed Book G: 25, 34. The circumstances of this purchase and immediate sale are unusual and continue to be investigated. The difference in the purchase/sale prices and the wording of Morris's purchase document suggests that he may have bought only a partial interest (from Warren V. Stewart and wife Ann E.), and that he or Miranda may have held a partial interest of their own prior to the first transaction.

[11]   Two military enrollments for individuals named Nathaniel Morris have been found for the Civil War era, but neither can be definitely attached to him. The two are: (1) no. 3198, enlistement 1 November 1863 at Fayette, with service in Co. C, 1st Prov. Regt., E.M.M., Co. H, 46th Regt., E.M.M., Co. L, 8th MSM Cav. Vols., ad Co. A, 9th MSM Cav. Vols.; and (2) no. 3198-C, enlistment 1862, age 31, Co. B, 2d Inf. CSA. See "Missouri, Adjutant General's Office, Military Records, General Index Files for Seminole, Mexican and Civil Waqrs, 1837-1865," Family History Library (FHL), Salt Lake City.

Additionally, there exists and 1865-66 militia index for Missouri, arranged by county. Nathaniel Morris is not found there. See FHL microcopy 1204772. The author thanks the NGSQ reviewers of this manuscript for suggesting this source.

[–?--] Taylor

This unknown male died before August 1835, leaving a modest estate with several slaves. He left a minor, Theodore, for whom annual accounts were posted by his guardian, Francis J. Bevan, between August 1836 and May 1842. Court proceedings intimate that Theodore lived in the town of Pinckney.[12] On 9 December 1841, he married Tobellah Owsley in a ceremony performed by the Reverend John Anderson.[13] That record does not cite him as a minor. The implication is that Theodore came of age between November 1841 (when Bevan filed that year's annual account) and May 1842 (when the final guardianship account was filed). None of the records relating to this guardianship identify the parent from whom Theodore presumably inherited. None mention any other relative. No similar record was created for Miranda, who was likewise a minor in the period in which this guardianship transpired.

Daniel Taylor

Of Bridgeport township at the time of the 1840 census, Daniel was said to be in his nineties, sharing a home with a female in her sixties. The family included no other occupant – particularly no female child in the two-to-fifteen category as Miranda would have been.[14] Revolutionary War pension files reveal that Daniel had been a soldier of the Virginia line. Born in New Jersey, about forty miles from New York City, he had moved with his family to Virginia and lived in Frederick and Greenbrier counties. About 1800, he migrated westward to Bardstown, Kentucky. From there he moved, before 1830, to Montgomery County, Missouri (later Warren), where he applied for his pension in May 1833. No mention is made of a wife or a daughter at that time.[15] As a pensioner, he left no property to probate.

Elizabeth Taylor

Possibly a widow, Elizabeth of Bridgeport was in her thirties in 1840, living with a small boy and girl, both under five years, and a man said to be over one hundred. On the basis of age, Elizabeth would seem to be a viable candidate for Miranda's mother, but there is no adolescent female of Miranda's age living with Elizabeth.[16]

---

[12]   Warren Co. Probate Book A: 173, 250; see also pp. 139, 217, 250, 34`, and 379.

[13]   Warren Co. Marr. Book A: 79.

[14]   1840 U.S. cens., Warren Co., p. 153.

[15]   Virgil D. White, *Genealogical Abstracts of Revolutionary War Pension Files*, 4 vols. (Waynesboro, Tenn.: National Historical Publishing Co., 1992), 3: 3426; 1830 U.S. Cens., Montgomery Co., Mo., Lower Lautre twp., p. 207.

[16]   1840 U.S. cens., Warren Co., p. 152.

Fountain Taylor

This young man of Hickory Grove township was one of seven Taylor heads of household enumerated on the 1840 census. Aged fifteen to twenty, with a wife aged twenty to thirty and no children, Fountain can be eliminated as a possible father of Miranda – although he might remain in consideration as a potential brother.[17] On 12 September 1839, he wed one Delilah McCann before Joseph Nichols, a Missionary Baptist minister at Warrenton. The county's record of that marriage states "groom underage, father present and consenting."[18]

Jesse Taylor

A non-testamentary estate was probated for Jesse Taylor in May 1840. A guardian was appointed for his son, William W., who was said to be "a minor, abandoned by his father for more than six months."[19] No mention is made of a child Miranda being left in similar circumstances.

Roger Taylor

This householder of Hickory Grove, aged fifty to sixty, was of appropriate age to qualify for Miranda's father. However, his dwelling housed only one female (of his same age bracket) and two young males (aged ten to fifteen and twenty to thirty). No teenaged females were recorded.[20] Moreover, his estate was probated in Warren County; and Miranda is not named amid the lengthy list of his heirs that included the following:[21]

> Hannah Taylor, widow
> William O. Ross and wife Lucinda
> Benajah English and wife Sarah S.
> James T. [F.?] Taylor
> Robert J. Huston and wife Caroline
> Colby H. Taylor
> Samuel D. Taylor
> John A. Woolfolte[?], attorney-in-fact of Matilda Woolfocte[?], late Matilda
>   Taylor
> Daniel McFarland and wife Letitia, late Letitia Taylor
> W. G. Porter, husband of the deceased Eleanor Porter, late Eleanor Taylor (and
>   guardian of Martha V. and Eleanor M. C. Porter, their infants)
> William R. Taylor, infant heir over age fourteen
> Jacob F. Taylor, infant heir over age fourteen

---

[17]   1840 U.S. cens., Warren Co., p. 170.
[18]   Warren Co., Marr. Book A: 56.
[19]   Warren Co., Probate Book A: 237.
[20]   1840 U.S. cens., Warren Co., p. 170.
[21]   Warren Co., Probate Book A: 446, 455, 482, 496.

Thomas Taylor

This young man, in his twenties, lived alone in the town of Warrenton in 1840.[22] He was hardly of the right age to be the father of Miranda, although he might remain a candidate for brother or other relative.

Vincent Taylor

The Hickory Grove family of Vincent Taylor was the only 1840 household with a female of appropriate age. Vincent and his apparent wife were both between forty and fifty years. Four boys ranged from five to fifteen. Three girls were of compatible age with Miranda (ten to fifteen), while a fourth was between fifteen and twenty.[23] Given the children's ages, Vincent's marriage would seem to antedate the 1833 creation of the county. His intestate probate file, begun 1 May 1865, names only creditors (including one Eli P. Taylor), purchasers of estate goods, and his widow Cecilia J. Taylor, who received final distribution of the resulting ten dollars.[24]

Washington Taylor

Living in Elk Horn township, Washington Taylor and his apparent wife were both recorded as twenty to thirty years of age, with two boys under the age of five.[25] Clearly, this family could be excluded also.

Focusing the search

Nine Taylor families could be placed in Warren County during the decade Miranda came of age and married there. Presuming that her parents had settled the region prior to the 1840 census, then only one of the nine possibilities was viable: the Vincent Taylors of Hickory Grove. Geographically, the middle-aged Vincent might also be linked with two other males of the Hickory Grove township: Roger Taylor (aged fifty to sixty) and Fountain Taylor (fifteen to twenty). Because Fountain's 1839 marriage record explicitly says that he was a minor and that his father attended the wedding, it might be hypothesized that either Vincent or Roger was that unnamed father.

Focusing the search upon Vincent produced numerous associational, geographic, and migratory links with Miranda – almost all centering upon the McCann family into which Vincent married.

---

[22]   1840 U.S. cens., Warren Co., p. 172.
[23]   1840 U.S. cens., Warren Co., p 170.
[24]   Warren Co. Probate Book B: 267,294; also Warren Co. Loose Paper Probate File for Vincent Taylor. Regarding the involvement of Eli in Vincent's estate, note that Miranda named a son Eli.
[25]   Warren Co., Probate Book B: 172.

Associational links

On 6 November 1839, a Missionary Baptist minister named Joseph Nichols performed the Warrenton wedding of Vincent to the widow Mary McCann.[26] (Nichols was the same preacher who had officiated when Fountain Taylor married Delilah McCann on 12 September 1839, in the presence of Fountain's unidentified father.[27]) Assuming Vincent's 1839 bride to be the adult female in his 1840 home (aged forty to fifty), then she should not be the mother of Miranda, who was born circa 1826-28.

The estate of Mary's first husband, Neal McCann, had gone to probate in Warren County in May 1836. Their children and heirs are identified in the proceedings, and several have marriages recorded in Warren. In brief:[28]

McCann Child	Spouse	Marriage Date	Officiating Party
Salama	[-?-] Skinner	before 1836	
Jesse[29]	Thalba Williams	17 May 1836	John P. Shaw, J.P.
Rhoda	Elihu Cooper	before 1836	
Matilda[30]	William Cook	10 April 1836	John P. Shaw, J.P.
Polly[31]	Lawrence Lankford	14 July 1836	Thos. Bowen, Bapt. Min.
Delilah[32]	Fountain Taylor	12 Sep 1839	Jos. Nichols, Bapt. Min.
Lewis[33]	Mary Ann Johnson	28 Nov 1844	A. S. Wood, J.P.
Sarah[34]	Jesse Cartwright	27 May 1841	Jos. Nichols, Bapt. Min.
Rhuhama[35]	Porter Neal	ca. 1840-50[36]	

Two of the factors outlined in this table support the hypothesis that Miranda belongs to the family of Vincent Taylor – i.e.:

o At the time of the 1840 census, two of the McCann girls remained unmarried and probably followed their mother into Vincent's household. They should account for two of the females aged ten to fifteen, leaving one remaining

---

[26]   Warren Co., Marr. Book A: 59.

[27]   Warren Co., Marr Book A: 56.

[28]   Warren Co., Probate Book A: 74, 108, 128. Unless otherwise stated, data given in the above table for the McCann children and heirs are from this probate record.

[29]   Warren Co., Marr. Book A: 24.

[30]   Warren Co., Marr. Book A: 22. This record states "bride underage, [married] by consent of her parents." Thus, it would seem that Neal McCann died between the 10 April 1836 marriage and the May 1836 opening of his probate.

[31]   Warren Co., Marr. Book A: 24.

[32]   Warren Co., Marr. Book A: 56.

[33]   Warren Co., Marr. Book A: 113.

[34]   Warren Co., Marr. Book A: 73.

[35]   Family record of Edmund James Bonham.

[36]   Rhuhama died before 1850, at which time her husband is enumerated in the household of Jesse and Sarah (McCann) Cartwright; see 1850 U.S. cens., pop. sch., Grant Co., Wis., dist. 24, p. 29, dwell. 403, fam. 409. Rhuhama is not found on the mortality schedule of that 1850 census. Thus, she *possibly* died before 1 June 1849, as all deaths between that date and 1 June 1850 were *supposed* to be recorded on the mortality schedule.

40

possibility for Miranda.

o The Baptist minister who officiated at the 1836 marriage of Polly McCann to Lawrence Lankford was the same minister who served Miranda Taylor and Nathaniel Morris in 1847. By implication, either Miranda or Nathaniel attended the same church as Polly McCann, stepdaughter of Vincent Taylor.

Geographic links

Two sets of circumstances offer potential to test geographic links between Vincent Taylor and Miranda (Taylor) Morris. The first considers Vincent's origins; the second, his place of residence in Warren County.

According to the 1850 census of Warren, the fifty-two-year-old Vincent (like Miranda) was born in Virginia. A farmer and apparently a widower again, he shared his home with the seventeen-year-old Stephen B. Taylor, also born in Virginia.[37] Agreeable to this data, the 1830 census shows no Vincent Taylor in Missouri. But two men of this name were householders in the Old Dominion:

Fauquier County, Virginia, 1830, p. 454

Vincent Taylor	1 male	50-59	1 female	50-59
	3 males	0-5	1 female	20-29

King and Queen County, Virginia, 1830, p. 289[38]

Vincent Taylor	1 male	30-39	1 female	30-39
	1 male	20-29	2 females	5-9
	1 male	10-14	1 female	0-5
	1 male	0-5		

The latter family's composition and age data are compatible with the family that removed to Missouri – including a girl of age corresponding to Miranda. Vincent of King and Queen does not appear on that county's enumeration in 1840. Meanwhile, when the first town lots were sold in Warrenton, Missouri, in January 1836, the original purchasers included Vincent Taylor.[39] Whether his first wife accompanied him to Missouri is uncertain. In the extant land records of that county, he first appears as a grantor on 19 January 1839 – ten months before his remarriage; no wife participated in that January sale or subsequently relinquished her dower.[40]

No document directly states the community in which Miranda resided with her husband; nor does any state how close their residence was to that of Vincent Taylor.

---

[37]   1850 U.S. cens., pop. sch., Warren Co., 99th dist., p. 40, dwell. 189, fam. 199.

[38]   Next-door to this Vincent Taylor is the household of Caleb Taylor, aged sixty to sixty-nine – i.e., old enough to be Vincent Taylor's father.

[39]   *History of St. Charles, Montgomery, and Warren Counties, Missouri* (1885; reprinted, St. Louis: Paul V. Cochrane, 1969), 1068. The extant land records of Warren Co. do not begin until 1838, two years after the original town lots were sold.

[40]   Warren Co., Warrantee Deed Book B: 326, and Mortgage Book C: 324.

However, the purchase and sale of land that Nathaniel Morris made in January 1855 and a conveyance executed soon after by Vincent Taylor provide a common locus for the households. Warren County in the 1850s sprawled across some three hundred and ten square miles; yet the Morris land and the Taylor land lay less than a mile apart. (See figure 1.) The key documents that testify to their geographic proximity are these:

20 January 1855
Nathaniel Morris and wife Miranda sell 40 acres of land in Morris County, described as northeast quarter of southwest quarter of section 5, township 47 north, range 2 west.[41]

8 March 1855
Vincent Taylor (no wife)[42] sells 37.5 acres described as northeast quarter of southeast quarter of section 7, township 47 north, range 2 west; also 2.5 acres lying in adjoining section 8, township 47 north, range 2 west.[43]

A long-standing association with this township 47, range 2, neighborhood is suggested for Vincent by one other record – one that could be misleading if his connection to the McCanns was not known. Sued for debt in the wake of the worldwide financial crash of 1837 – a crisis that extended into the mid-1840s – Vincent and wife Mary were forced in 1842 to sell a tract of land described as 237.40 acres in section 13, township 47, range 3, and section 18, township 47, range 2. The purchaser was Ephraim Riddle. In April 1845, Fountain Taylor executed a deed in which he is cited as selling the exact same property to Ephraim Riddle.[44]

It is tempting to deduce, from this information, some familial connection between Vincent and Fountain Taylor; but a more thorough study of the deed records reveals that the property and the connection was a McCann one. Similar conveyances for this tract are found for "Lewis D. McCann and Maryann his wife" to Ephraim Riddle; for Jesse McCann to Riddle; and for "Lawrence Langford and Elizabeth, his wife" to Riddle. Still more are found for "William Cook and Matilda Cook, [his] wife" to Jesse Cartwright; then from "Jessee Cartwright and Sarah Cartwright his wife" to Mathew H. Cartwright, "estate administrator," who conveyed it to Riddle. This chain of transactions, the last of which occurred in 1850, represents the disposal of the real property of Neal McCann. Vincent and Fountain Taylor participated in the conveyances only as husbands of two McCann heirs.[45]

---

41   Warren Co., Deed Book G: 34.
42   Vincent remarried before 1860, but the marriage record has not been found. The wife Cecilia, named as widow in his 1865 probate file, is enumerated with him in 1860 as Criscillia, age 35. Also in the household was Geminah [Jemima] J. Garrett, 15; Thomas W. Garrett, 11; Agatha Gile (or Gill), 80; and John Collins, a farm laborer. See 1860 U.S. cens. pop. sch., Warren Co., Elkhorn twp., p. 38, dwell. 61, fam. 61.The 1855 sale of land above may have marked his marriage and removal to the land or community of the new wife.
43   Warren Co., Deed Book G: 66.
44   Warren Co., Deed Books C: 324; D: 351, 535.
45   Warren Co. Deed Books C: 332, 403; E: 404; and F: 22.5 [sic], 32, 43.

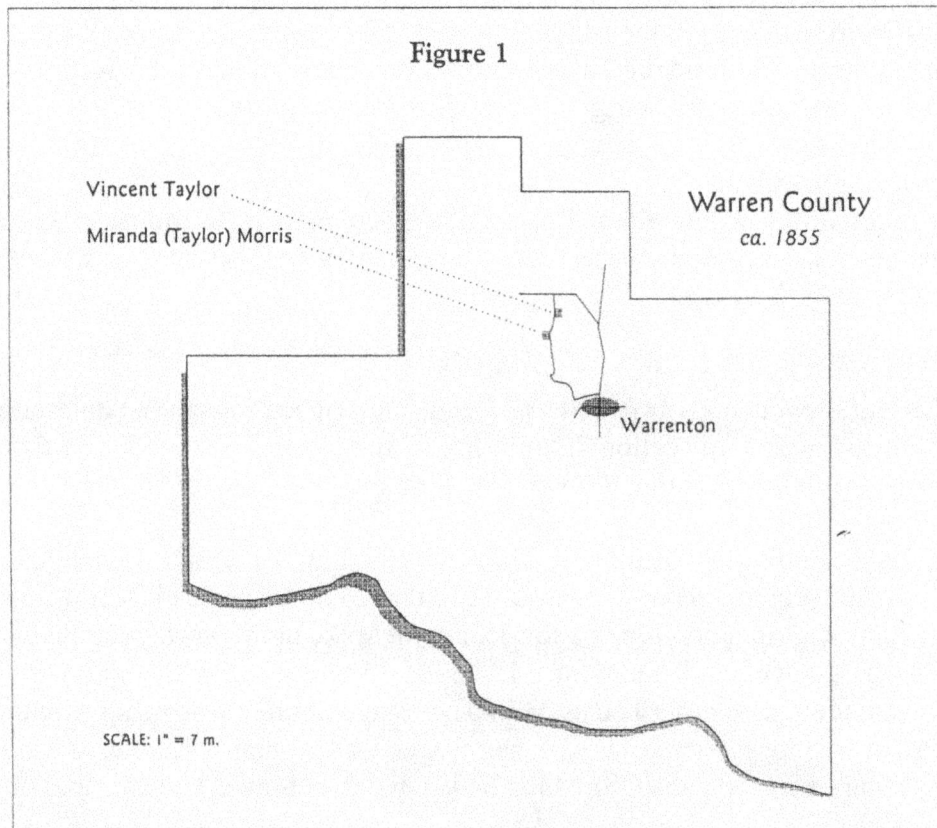

Figure 1

Warren County
ca. 1855

Vincent Taylor

Miranda (Taylor) Morris

Warrenton

SCALE: 1" = 7 m.

Migratory links

In the mid-1860s – concurrent perhaps with the deaths of Vincent Taylor (her proposed father) and Nathaniel Morris, her husband – Miranda moved with her children to Wisconsin. If the developing hypothesis is correct, that Miranda (Taylor) Morris is connected to the Taylor-McCann cluster, then members of that extended family should be found with her in the new locale. They were. In brief:

   o Fountain and Delilah (McCann) Taylor moved to Wisconsin around 1845. The 1850 census of Grant County cites a Missouri birth about 1842 for their second child and a Wisconsin birth about 1845 for the third.[46] Fountain and Delilah were still in the county in 1870, in the same vicinity as Miranda.[47]

   o Jesse and Sarah (McCann) Cartwright and William and Matilda (McCann) Cook also appear on the Grant enumeration of 1850, virtually next door to Fountain

---

[46]   1850 U.S. cens., pop. sch., Grant Co., Wis., dist. 24, p. 29, dwell. 402, fam. 408.

[47]   1870 U.S. cens., pop., sch., Grant Co., Wis., Potosi twp., p. 3, dwell. 18, fam. 18 (Miranda Morris) and Beetown, p. 16, dwell. 22, fam. 22 (Fountain Taylor). Beetown and Potosi townships are contiguous.

and Delilah. With the Cartwrights lived Porter Neal, widower of Rhuhama McCann.[48]

o William Cook and Jesse Cartwright were actually listed in absentia, in the Wisconsin households of their wives and children. Both men had gone to California in 1849. Cook died there in 1850. Jesse Cartwright, who was enumerated in California's Eldorado County in 1850, apparently died there as well. In 1853, his widow Sarah (McCann) married her late sister's husband, Porter Neal. Meanwhile, Cook's widow Matilda (McCann) married James Bonham, formerly of Pike County.[49]

o After Matilda (Taylor) Morris and her children joined the Taylor-McCann family in Wisconsin, Miranda's son William wed Anna Bonham, daughter of James and Matilda (McCann) Bonham. With James, Matilda, William, Anna, and other members of this extended family (including Edmund James Bonham, who compiled a family account in 1920), Miranda migrated to Iowa and Kansas.[50]

Conclusions

No known documentary evidence exists by which the parentage of Miranda (Taylor) Morris can be directly proved. However, the indirect evidence is compelling. She emerged in Warren County, Missouri, as a young bride in 1847. The only area family of her surname, of compatible age and family composition, was that of Vincent Taylor. The only land that she and her husband owned was located within a mile of Vincent's land. As a widow in need of a support network, after Vincent and her husband died, she relocated in Grant County, Wisconsin – amid Vincent's stepchildren, who were surely her own stepsisters. There, her son married the daughter of Vincent's stepdaughter. And from there, she followed the stepkin across two more states.

Miranda's behavior, Miranda's choices, are logical and convincing. Traditional literature favors accounts of families split asunder by remarriages and incompatible step-relationships. Less publicized are the marital kinships that strengthened families, extended them, and – consequently – expanded the options that genealogists must consider. Miranda (Taylor) Morris makes this point.

[48] 1850 U.S. cens., pop. sch., Grant Co., Wis., dist. 24, p. 29, dwells. 403, 407, fams. 409, 413.
[49] For the Neal-Cartwright marriage, see Grant Co. Marr. Book 1: 148. For Cook's death and his widow's remarriage to Bonham, see Family Records of Edmund James Bonham, 1920; and Emmet L. Smith, *Bonham, 1631-1908* (Chicago: Privately printed, 1908), 33. See also 1850 U.S. cens., pop. sch., Eldorado Co., Calif., p. 269.
[50] Family Record of Edmund James Bonham, 1920.

Chapter 6

A Census Consensus:
1840 in Warren County, Missouri[1]

Even though the 1840 federal and state censuses for Missouri name only heads of household, a methodical evaluation of the data can nonetheless point to the identity and parentage of the unnamed children within.

Federal censuses prior to 1850 are often exercises in frustration for genealogists. The family names we so desire to learn about are there in tantalizing array, and yet family members remain elusively anonymous. What can be done with statistical categories that could include cousins, nephews, adopted children, hired hands, and even strangers? By combining the pre-1850census listings with data from other sources, it is often possible to define, identify, or at least categorize family members with a reasonably high probability. Less commonly – as in the present case – the researcher may have a valuable boon: *two* censuses for the same year, with slightly different statistical categories.

An earlier study of the parentage of Miranda Taylor of Warren County, Missouri, shows that Miranda (born about 1826-28) and Stephen Bernard Taylor (born about 1833) were children of Vincent Taylor, a farmer born in Virginia.[2] In addition, Eli P. Taylor (born about 1829) is very likely another son of Vincent.[3] The present study deals with yet-another child of Vincent Taylor and his first wife.

In 1840, two separate enumerations were made of Missouri – one federal and one state. The returns for Warren county offer the following data for children in the Vincent Taylor household:

---

[1]   "A Census Concensus, 1840, Warren County, Missouri," *The National Genealogical Society Quarterly*, Vol 85, #2, June 1997, pp 116-119.

[2]   William M. Litchman, "Widows, Stepkin, and Support Networks: Clues to the Unknown Father of Miranda (taylor) Morris, *NGS Quarterly* 94 (March 1996): 5-15. For Miranda and Vincent, see especially 1850 U.S. cens., Warren County, Missouri, pop. sch., dist. 99, p. 40, dwell. 189, fam. 199; 1860 U.S. cens., Warren County, pop. sch., Campbranch twp, p. 182, dwell. 61, fam. 61; 1870 U.S. cens., Warren County, pop. sch., Elk Horn twp, p. 735, dwell. 347, fam. 304; and 1880 U.S. cens., Warren County, pop. sch., Elkhorn twp North of Bluehill Road, p. 696, dwell. 3, fam. 3.

[3]   1850 U.S. cens., Warren County, pop. sch., dist. 99, p. 66, dwell. 586, fam.586; 1860 U.S. cens., Warren County, pop. sch., Campbranch twp, p. 182, dwell. 362, fam. 362; 1880 U.S. cens., Grant County, Wis., pop. sch., Beetown Village, p. 34, dwell. 247, fam. 247. Eli is listed as a debtor in the Vincent Taylor estate settlement, Warren County Loose Probate Files (microfilmed, accessible through card index on-site), Recorder's Office, Warrenton.

Gender	No.	Federal	No.	State
boys/girls	0	0-5		
boys	3	5-10		
boys			3	0-10
boys	1	10-15		
girls	3	10-15		
girls	1	15-20		
boys			1	10-18
girls			4	10-18
Total [school-age] children			7	5-16

The individual listings for the federal and state censuses add up to the same number of children: four boys and four girls. However, only seven of the children are listed in the 5-16 category in the state-census total. Seven also appear in the under-15 category of the federal return – four boys and *three* girls. Thus, the eighth child must have been a girl over 16 and under 18 – that is, exactly 17. Assuming that the census taker followed his instructions and recorded the age of each family member as of the official census date, 1 June 1840 (and did so correctly), then the girl had to have been born between 2 June 1822 and 1 June 1823.

To focus temporarily on the girls: the Miranda Taylor study identifies the three girls aged 10-15 as Miranda Taylor (daughter of Vincent by his first wife) and two McCann daughters of Vincent's second wife, the widow Mary McCann.[4] The older girl remains unidentified in the study of Miranda. Can she be identified by a close analysis and correlation of the census records?

Because of this child's age in 1840, she likely married within the next few years. Two Taylor women of Warren County wed in the following decade: Catherine Taylor married William Brisco, 16 March 1843,[5] and Miranda Taylor married Nathaniel Morris, 28 October 1847.[6] Miranda has been reconstructed in detail in the prior article, but Catherine remained unattached to any Taylor parents.

Assigning Catherine to a Taylor family began with a survey of all Taylors in the area of her marriage. As detailed in the prior paper: the 1840 census of Warren County identifies six Taylor households, and auxiliary county records identify three other adult Taylor males who created local records of some type between 1835 and 1843.[7] Of all these, only two had girls in 1840: (a) Vincent, whose data appear on the prior page; and (b) Elizabeth, whose two children consisted of a boy under 5 and a girl under 5.[8]

---

[4] Litchman, "Widows, Stepkin, and Support Networks," 22-27.

[5] Warren Co., Marr. Book A: 91.

[6] Warren Co., Marr. Book B: 150.

[7] Litchman, *Op. Cit.*

[8] 1840 U.S. cens., Warren County, pop. sch., p 152, line 25.

Thus, even though the 1840 federal and state censuses for Missouri name only heads of households, a methodical evaluation of the data can nonetheless point to the identity and parentage of the unnamed children within. In this case, the oldest female child in the Vincent Taylor family was logically Catherine, for the following reasons:

Only one unidentified Taylor female appears in the county's marriage records of 1840-50.

The pair of censuses point to only one female in a Taylor household who would have been of marriageable age in the decade 1840-50 (assuming that the family gave the data correctly and the enumerator recorded it correctly).

The age of that female, which can be set precisely at 17, is an appropriate age for a female who married three years later.

This conclusion, of course, rests on the premise that no teenage Taylor female resided in any household of a different surname – a premise that the odds favor but one that could be faulty nonetheless. In the present case, one other fact adds the additional weight needed to justify the conclusion: *both Miranda and Catherine were married by the same minister* – Thomas Bowen – suggesting strongly that they were affiliated with the same neighborhood church. Given the rural nature of their society and the small congregations that prevailed there, the odds that Vincent Taylor and his wife gave a home to a young female of another family, while a nearby household of a different surname had an unattached Taylor girl of the same age, are too slim to consider without supporting evidence. In this case, all the evidence is circumstantial, but all of it points to a conclusion that is compatible with prevailing social habits. Until and unless specifically disproved, Catherine can be accepted as the unnamed, 17-year-old daughter of Vincent in 1840.[9]

Postscript

With many research problems of this type, the research potential ends here – years of followup reveal nothing more. At other times records surface to confirm or refute the hypothesis. Catherine Taylor presents one of those situations also, as well as another lesson for the student of genealogy.

The widespread microfilming of source materials and their accessibility through the Family History Centers of the Church of Jesus Christ of Latter-day Saints means that extensive research can be done without the expense of on-site visits. All good genealogists are aware that on-site work is still wise, even when microfilmed records appear "complete," because unfilmed records exist in many locales. Yet, follow-up trips to the local courthouse often yield nothing more than the materials already used.

That seemed to be the case with the Catherine Taylor problem. Amid the previous work on Miranda, local researchers had been employed to comb the courthouse for unfilmed materials. Several unfilmed probate packets for the Taylors were found, copied, and studied. None yielded a list of Vincent Taylor's children or heirs. After the present article had been accepted for publication the author scheduled a personal trip to Warren County, Missouri – hoping that a third search of courthouse materials would turn up something previously

---

[9]   Neither Catherine nor her husband have been located anywhere on 1850 and later censuses, for confirmation of the age extrapolated from 1840 census data.

missed. It did: an old volume of probate-related records that combined Will Books A, B, and C (1833-1869). There, on page 369 of Book C – but not in the packet of original probate papers – appears a document created and filed by Cecelia Taylor, widow (and third wife) of Vincent, on 6 May 1865, shortly after Vincent's death. Included is a list of his heirs (apparently all by his first wife): Miranda, Eli, Fountain, Bernard, and Catherine Taylor.

This document reads:

"State of Missouri, County of Warren: I, Cecelia J. Taylor, do swear to the best of my knowledge and belief that Vincent Taylor died without a will, that Fountain Taylor, Wisconsin; Kety Briscoe, Kentucky; Eli Taylor, Wisconsin; Bernard Taylor, Illinois; Muranda Morris, Wisconsin; are all the heirs of said deceased, that I will make a perfect inventory of and faithfully administer all the estate of said deceased, and pay all the debts as far as the assets will extend & the law direct, & account for & pay all assets which shall come to my possession or knowledge. Subscribed & sworn to before me this 6th day of May 1865. Albert P. Frowein, Clerk. Filed May 6th, 1865." [Will Record, Books A, B, C, June 1833-Apr 1869, Warren County, Missouri, p. 369 (Vol. C).]

In this one document, the parentage of Miranda, Fountain, Eli, Bernard, and Catherine are all proved by as direct a witness as can reasonably be found. It is satisfying to know how accurately the circumstantial evidence predicted this result. Perhaps one day Catherine will be found.

Chapter 7

A Leap of Faith:
The Dunlap–Pattison Family of Maghera,
Northern Ireland (1740-1820)[1]

If only all of our ancestors were kings and queens! Ordinary families always provide challenges. Families of Irish origin provide extra special challenges and Northern Irish families can try the patience of even the most dedicated family historians. Perhaps the most difficult part of coming to terms with family research in Ireland is finding the specific village or townland from which the family emigrated to North America.

Slaghtybogy, near Maghera, County Derry, is given in an eighteenth century hand-made family book as the townland of origin of the Dunlap-Pattison family. This book also details the structure of the family and their emigration from Ulster to America,[2] (see Figure 1). But the paucity of Ulster documents has forced a broadening of scope. The purpose of this article is to describe the living conditions of the Dunlap-Pattison family that sent them to America.

Setting the economic stage for our story, a "Plantation" scheme was instituted by the English King James I in about 1609,[3] in which the lands of Ireland, especially in Ulster, were offered to the London crafts guilds at a nominal rent. Recurring rebellions of the Irish were costing the English crown investment money as well as lost income. The plan behind this was that the guilds would find agents to recruit patriotic Scotsmen and northern Englishmen to bring their families to settle in Ireland. By this means the rebellious Irish population would be diluted and subdued, the guilds would also glean a profit by the rents gathered by their agents and the emigrants would find a better economic life.

Each layer of renters would subdivide their holding, rent smaller and smaller parcels of land for higher and higher rents until at the lowest level one would find the actual user of the land, the farmer, the tiller of the soil. The further up the ladder one went, the more

---

[1]   "A Leap of Faith: The Dunlap–Pattison Family of Maghera, Northern Ireland (1740-1820)," *The Genealogical Journal*, Vol 31, #2, 2003, pp 67-75.

[2]   William M. Litchman, "Family Records of William Dunlap of Ireland and Charleston Carlisle, and Rutland, New York," *New York Genealogical and Biographical Record*, 125, #1, January 1994, pp 8-12, and 125, #2, April 1994, pp 102-105.

[3]   James G. Ryan, *Irish Records: Sources for Family & Local History*, (Salt Lake City, (UT): Ancestry Publishing 1988), p. 113.

removed from the land the landlord became (in general).[4]

By the early eighteenth century, with the plantation program well underway, Ireland was an open country for the immigration of Scots, including, most likely, the ancestors of this Dunlap-Pattison family. There was pressure at home from increasing rents and the lack of market for home-made goods.[5] It must have been very inviting for families to come to Ireland, acquire land (through paying rents, of course) and then to improve themselves financially. Certainly, the rebellions of the native Irish were not part of the publicity!

Two benchmark dates for the family provide the time period for records to seek in fleshing out this family's Ulster experience: 13 March 1790, the birth date for William Dunlap, eldest known child[6] of Joseph Dunlap and Elizabeth Arbuthnot,[7] allows us to extrapolate the first, an approximate beginning date, and 8 May 1792,[8] the voyage of the *Tristram* taking the family to America is the second (providing closure).

The average age for men (25) and women (22) at marriage,[9] and the assumption that all marriages occurred during the year preceding the birth of the first child give us the framework for our extrapolation. Using these assumptions, Joseph and Elizabeth were probably married in 1789, Joseph was probably born in 1764, William, sr, and Mariann were probably married in about 1763, and William, sr, was probably born no later than about 1738 and Mariann Pattison about three years later.

Many Maghera-area Scots families came from County Ayr[10] and there are certainly Dunlap and Pattison families present in that county throughout the 1700s.

No appropriate christenings are found for Joseph (ca 1764), William (April 1770), or Sarah Dunlap (1775-1780), nor are there baptisms for Mariann Pattison (ca 1741), William Pattison (ca 1746), or Matthew Pattison (ca 1748).[11] William Dunlap is such a common name that it is impossible to know if our William is in the records. No marriage for Joseph and Margaret Pattison is found.

---

[4] Jonathan Bardon, *A History of Ulster*, (Belfast, (NI): The Blackstaff Press, first published 1992, 1996 reprint), chapters 5 and 7.

[5] R. J. Dickson, *Ulster Emigration to Colonial America 1718-1775*, (Belfast (NI): Ulster Historical Foundation, first published 1966, fourth reprint by UHF, 2001), chapter 1.

[6] The birth dates for all of their children are found in the loose paper file associated with the probate records for the estate of Joseph Dunlap, Montgomery county, New York.

[7] Arthur C. M. Kelly, *Baptism Record of Caughnawaga Reformed Church, Fonda, NY, 1758-1899*, (Rhinebeck (NY): Privately published, n.d.). This source gives Elizabeth's maiden name: "year 1796; day -; month -; father Joseph Dunlap; mother Elizabeth Orbuthnot; item number 1893; child's name Jean; born 9 March 1795; no sponsors listed."

[8] *The Londonderry Journal*, 1 May 1792, #1506, page 1, column 4.

[9] William M. Litchman, "Shaving with Occam's Razor: A Proposed Descendancy for Edward Warren of Fox Island, Newfoundland," Part I, *The Newfoundland Ancestor*, Vol. 17, #4, pp. 185-194.

[10] Rev. S. Sidlow McFarland, *Presbyterianism in Maghera: A Social and Congregational History*, (n.p., n.d.), p. 24.

[11] Search of the Old Parochial Registers of Scotland, the "Scottish Church Records" data base, a part of Family Search, a data-search program found at Family History Centers, branch libraries of the Family History Library, Salt Lake City.

Table 1.

Schematic of the Family of Joseph and Margaret Pattison
of Slaghtybogy, Parish of Maghera, County Derry (1716-1820)

Joseph Pattison (b ca 1716) m Margaret (—) before 1740 X[1741]
    Children:
    1.   Mariann (b ca 1743, d ca 1790) X(b ca 1741, d ca 1790)
        m William Dunlap (b ca 1740, d ca 1805-10) X (b ca 1738...
      Children:
      i. Joseph (b ca 1765, d July 1802)
          m Elizabeth Arbuthnot (ca 1789)
        Children:
            a. William (b March 1790)
            b. Robert (b September 1792)
            c. Jane/Jean (b March 1795)
            d. Mary Ann (b June 1797)
            e. Nancy (b June 1800)
            f. Joseph (b December 1802)
      ii. William (b April 1770, d 1833)
          m Elizabeth Middleton (14 February 1799, d September 1819)
          a. Andrew (b February 1801)
          b. Mariann (b April 1802)
          c. Margaret (b October 1803)
          d. William Middleton (b February 1805)
          e. John (b June 1806, d November 1815)
          f. Sarah (b February 1809)
          g. Elizabeth (b November 1810)
          i. Susannah (b March 1812)
          j. Amelia (b November 1813)
          k. Joseph Pattison (b January 1814)
          l. John M. (b February 1818)
          m. Harriet (b August 1819)
      iii. Sarah (b ca 1775-80, d ca 1840-50)
          m James Carey (1798, d ca 1827)
      iv. Child (b and d ca 1790)
    2.   William (b ca 1747, d aft 1821)
    3.   Matthew (b ca 1749, d bef 1823)

The townland of Slaghtybogy was the exclusive property of the Vintner's company and the first known renter was John Elliott.[12] Any further sub-renting of the land would have had to be through him or his successors and heirs. The Elliott family continued to control the townland for quite a number of years.[13] Thomas Connolly, speaker of the Irish House of Commons, purchased the lease in the mid 1700s and his heirs continued there for many years thereafter.

Josh (Joseph?) Paddyson is listed as a resident of the Parish of Maghera in 1740, Joseph Patterson in 1796,[14] and the name of Joseph Pattison [not Patterson] is found as a resident of Magherafelt,[15] a small community about 10 miles from Maghera, and a part of the Salter's plantation in 1766.

Harlan Page Dunlap about 1905 stated that William Dunlap, sr, married "in Ireland, Mary Ann, daughter of Joseph and Margaret Patterson [sic]."[16] One Dunlap infant and the mother died and were buried in the "churchyard at Maghera" prior to the departure of the family in 1792.[17]

There were two churches at Maghera, both with burial grounds, one the ancient (ca 1200) church of St. Lurach (originally Catholic but by the late 1700s, Church of Ireland) and the other, the recently finished (1785) Presbyterian church. No relevant entries have been found in a search of the records of the Maghera Presbyterian Church.[18] There are no early records extant from the Church of Ireland in Maghera, nor were there any Dunlap names found on extant stones in the old St. Lurach graveyard[19] even though the Dunlap name was once known on those stones.[20]

Since very few (7.7%) of the residents of Slaghtybogy were Church of Ireland and

---

[12]   Vintners' Rent Roll for 1729 for Slatboglum, Public Records Office of Northern Ireland [PRONI], Belfast, Film D/2094/29.

[13]   Vintners' Rent Roll for November 1774 and May 1775, Slattabogy, PRONI Film D/2094/50. Vintners' Rent Roll for November 1775 and May 1776, Slattabogy, PRONI Film D/2094/50. Rent Roll, Slattobogy, Manor of Vintners', County Londonderry, PRONI Film D/2094/75. Rent Roll, Slatabogy, Manor of Vintners', County Londonderry, PRONI Film D/2094/78.

[14]   Personal letter from Thinet Bell, Magherafelt, Derry, Northern Ireland, dated 11 January 2003, in possession of William M. Litchman, giving extracts of the 1740 Protestant Householders' List (John Dunlap, Parish of Killyleagh; Josh [Joseph?] Paddyson and John Padyson, Parish of Maghera); the 1796 Flax Premium List for the Parish of Maghera, Joseph Patterson.

[15]   W. H. Maitland, *History of Magherafelt*, (Londonderry (NI): Moyola Books, first published 1916, this edition 1988, reprinted 1991), pp. 9-11, showing the "Parliamentary Return as to the Religious Denomination of the families in each parish in Ireland:" population of Magherafelt, 1766.

[16]   Harlan Page Dunlap, holographic statement in possession of the author. It was published verbatim in R. A. Oakes, *Genealotical and Family History of the County of Jefferson, New York*, (New York: The Lewis Publishing Company, 1905), Vol. I, pp. 450-452."

[17]   Litchman, "Family Records ...", op. cit.

[18]   Records of the Maghera Parish Church (Church of Ireland), 1785-1800, PRONI Film MIC/1/20.

[19]   Personal observation by the author during a trip to Maghera in July 2002.

[20]   Angélique Day and Patrick McWilliams, eds., *Ordnance Survey Memoirs of Ireland, Volume eighteen, Parishes of Country Londonderry V, 1830-1833, 1836-7, Maghera and Tamlaght O'Crilly*, (Dublin: The Institute of Irish Studies, 1993), pages 47-48.

nearly half (46%) were Presbyterian in 1831,[21] it seems most probable that the burial of Mariann Dunlap and her child took place in the Presbyterian churchyard. It also seems reasonable that the marriage of William Dunlap and Mariann Pattison took place in Slaghtybogy, at the bride's home, and the marriage of William's son, Joseph Dunlap, and Elizabeth Arbuthnot a generation later, possibly at the church.

Long leases "are the ruin of Ireland." These lengthy leases, sometimes for 999 years, were very successful early in the eighteenth century but they led to fixed rents at a time of rising values and prices. Tenants were then able to sublet very profitably. When primary leases finally ended, however, landlords were able to deal directly with the sub-tenants, especially in the "linen triangle" which included the Parish of Maghera. From 1753 to 1791, the number of houses paying hearth tax in Ulster almost doubled, giving northern landlords a unique opportunity to "set" or lease estates to increase their income.[22]

Toward the end of the eighteenth century, unrest, particularly first in Armagh and then spreading to other parts of Ulster, was growing more and more violent. Strife was mainly between individuals of the Protestant and Catholic faiths with atrocities committed on both sides.

Mariann Pattison had two brothers, William and Matthew, who emigrated to America some years prior to the Dunlap family,[23] probably in the wave of emigrations during the early 1770s.[24] "Economic crisis struck Ireland about 1770 and emigration rose to 10,000 per year at that time. Emigration abruptly ceased with the American Revolution but the economic crisis continued.[25]

To quote another writer,[26] "the loss of people from the northern part of Britain – from northern England, Scotland, and Northern Ireland – sent shock waves throughout the kingdom. People had been leaving these areas, particularly Ireland, since the end of the seventeenth century, but after 1763 the pattern and intensity of the migration changed. ... Sometimes whole neighborhoods of families and friends would leave in associations large enough to found their own wilderness communities. ... These sudden changes led to a crisis in the early 1770s that was described variously as a 'madness,' a 'contagion,' a 'frenzy,' and an 'evil' that would have 'ruinous' and 'dreadful' consequences."

Robert Johnston and several of his family members emigrated from Barley Hill, a farm in Slaghtybogy, to Pennsylvania in 1765.[27] They wrote letters back home extolling the virtues of their new country and describing their new life in detail.

William Dunlap (sr) was more likely to have been a merchant or tradesman in

[21] 1831 Census for Ireland, PRONI Film MIC/5A/8B.

[22] Jonathan Bardon, op. cit.

[23] Litchman, "Family Record ...," op. cit.

[24] R. J. Dickson, op. cit. Somerset county, New Jersey, Deed Book N, pp. 30-32, 6 October 1827, sheriff's sale of real property of William Patteson, described in a deed dated 29 August 1779.

[25] Jonathan Bardon, op. cit.

[26] Barbara De Wolfe, ed., *Discoveries of America: Personal Accounts of British Emigrants to North America during the Revolutionary Era*, (Cambridge (England): Cambridge University Press, 1997), page 6.

[27] Alun C. Davies, "'As Good a Country As Any Man Needs to Dwell In:' Letters from a Scotch-Irish Immigrant in Pennsilvania, 1766, 1767, and 1784," *Pennsylvania History*, Vol. L, #4, 1983, pages 313-322.

54

Maghera or a nearby community rather than a farmer like his father-in-law, Joseph Pattison. William (jr) was trained in surveying even though he desired to learn navigation for a career at sea.[28] His parents objected to the dangers of a nautical profession and he certainly became successful as a merchant and farmer in the new world. To be schooled in surveying, William (jr) would need to be apprenticed to a local surveyor or to attend a school to learn mathematics, geometry, and trigonometry. An apprenticeship is more likely since the state of schools in Northern Ireland at that time was deplorable.[29]

A coincidental event which might possibly have some relevance to the Dunlaps' urge to migrate involves the change in leadership at the local Presbyterian church. The Rev. David Smylie of Finvoy came to Maghera in 1739 and served faithfully for many years until ill-health forced him to retire in 1778. He died 23 July 1780. At that time the position was filled by Mr. John Glendy, ordained on 26 December 1778 as Mr. Smylie's assistant and successor.[30] He had "warm sympathies with the [Irish] revolutionary movement of the period" and had to go into hiding when that effort failed in 1798. It seems that "he was, in fact, a well-known if not an avowed rebel."[31] If the Dunlap and Pattison families weren't very sympathetic with the "revolutionary movement" and its methods, they may have been very uncomfortable in the community once Mr. Glendy was minister. With the increasing unrest of the people of Ireland, particularly in Ulster, the Dunlap family felt (probably with others) the need to emigrate to more propitious surroundings.

All these stresses (economic, social, and political) were wreaking havoc with personal lives. Thus, the advantages which drew the Dunlaps and Pattisons to Northern Ireland originally, deteriorated until the decision to emigrate to North America must have seemed a relief. It was made easier, of course, because William and Matthew Pattison were already established in New Jersey. It was to them that the little Dunlap family went upon landing at Philadelphia.

We can venture to guess that William Dunlap, sr, would have been about 52 years old at the time of his emigration from Ireland to America. It took a deal of bravery and courage to uproot his family from their home[32] in Ireland to make such a lengthy and dangerous journey.

It is apparent from the tone of the writings of William Dunlap[33] that the family were not indentured servants or redemptioners, as many were. Thus, they were able to pay their full passage, provide victuals for the passage, and have enough resources to sustain themselves through the first year(s) of living in the new world. The cost of passage averaged between 3 and 3.5 guineas[34] per adult passenger. Only William (Joseph's eldest, age 2) was

---

28   Harlan Page Dunlap, op. cit.

29   Graham Mashinney, *Shaw Mason's Maghera (1814) & Killelagh (1819): Extracts from A Statistical Account or Parochial Survey of Ireland*, (Draperstown (NI): Ballinascreen Historical Society), 1, page 30.

30   *A History of Congregations in the Presbyterian Church in Ireland 1610-1982*, (Belfast: Presbyterian Historical Society of Ireland, 1982), pages 619-623.

31   Eoin Walsh, *Famous Maghera Men*, (Belfast: Irish News Ltd., n.d.), page 19.

32   Day and McWilliams, op. cit., pages 52-53.

33   Litchman, "Family Record …," op. cit.

34   R. J. Dickson, op. cit.

a child so his passage was probably somewhat less. Sarah would have been 17, William, jr, 22. Thus, there would have been 5 adults and 1 child on this trip for a total passage amount of about 20 guineas or 21 pounds. They sailed on the Ship *Tristram*.[35]

> "For Newcastle & Philadelphia
> The fast sailing Ship
> TRISTRAM
> Burthen 300 tons
> G. A. Hallowell, Master
> Will be clear to sail for these Ports the 1st of April.

> The Tristram is particularly well adapted for the Passenger Trade. Those who wish to embrace this favourable Opportunity of going in a strong, new Ship, will do well to make speedy Application, as but 150 Passengers will be received. For Freight or Passages apply to Mr Rob. Cochran, Strabane; Mr. King Barton, Nn[36] Stewart; Mr. James King, Fintona; Mr. James Hamill, Coleraine; Mr. David Blair, Nn-Lemavady; or John Atchison Smyth and Co. Who engage that Plenty of Provisions and Water shall be laid in for the Voyage.

> N.B. The above vessell will sail the 8th of May, at which Time the Passengers are requested to be on Board."[37]

> "Schooner York, Stephenson, Liverpool
> Capt. Stephenson, on the 5th July, spoke the Tristram, from Derry for Philadelphia, with passengers, lat. 29, 20, long. 68"[38]

Latitude 29 degrees, 20 minutes is on a parallel with St. Augustine, Florida, and longitude 68 degrees, places the ship south and east but still fairly close to Bermuda, when they were only five days out from New Castle. Ships generally followed the trade winds in crossing the Atlantic by moving clockwise around a circle going east across the north and west across the mid-Atlantic. This is exactly the pattern suggested by that single "speaking" of the Tristram by the Schooner *York*.

> "The Ship Tristram, Capt. Hallowell, is arrived at New Castle from Londonderry, after a passage of 45 days with 150 passengers."[39]

> "A very considerable number of Irish emigrants have arrived in this and other states

---

[35]   Litchman, "Family Record ...," op. cit.

[36]   The abbreviation Nn stands for Newtown.

[37]   *The Londonderry Journal*, 1 May 1792, #1506, p. 1, col. 4, read from PRONI Film MIC/60/5. The same ad was run again on 8 May, #1507, p. 1, col. 4, but not after that.

[38]   *The Daily Advertiser*, New York, Mon., 9 July 1792, p. 3.

[39]   *The Daily Advertiser*, New York, Tue., 10 July 1792, p. 2. An identical statement was in *Dunlap's American Daily Advertiser*, Philadelphia, Tue., 10 July 1792, #4198, p. 2. The length of the trip was actually 47 days.

during the present month. Report says that the spirit of emigration is so prevalent in Ireland; especially in the northern and eastern [regions] that the lower and middling classes would universally remove to this side of the Atlantic, could they find ships to bring them off."[40]

With the successful arrival of the Dunlaps at Philadelphia, our story ends.

Chapter 8

Scattered Pieces:
Assembling a King and Queen County, Virginia,
Taylor Family from Scanty Records[1]

> The challenge of narrowing a migrating ancestor's point of origin to at
> least the county level can frustrate genealogists, especially if common
> surnames are involved. When researchers find the county and learn that
> its record losses are significant, they may admit defeat and never
> discover the treasure that may remain. Even when records are scarce,
> however, confidently identifying an ancestral family can be possible.

Fortunate is the genealogist who finds a record pinpointing a migrating ancestor's
place of origin. Luck doubles when the ancestral starting point is rich in records. Such
fortune, however, is unusual. Typical ancestors migrating in the eighteenth and nineteenth
centuries rarely recorded their origins more precisely than naming a colony, state, or nation.
In the case of ancestors who emigrated from Virginia – as did many settlers in the Midwest
and Southeast – researchers may be faced with an extreme poverty of records. "More than
40 percent of Virginia's county courts have suffered records losses" according to the Virginia
State Library and Archives, which also reported that "about half of those have lost all or
almost all of their records; the others have had less extensive but still significant losses."[2]

Vincent Taylor, an ancestor found in Missouri in the 1830s through the 1860s,
presented the above problems and more for researchers trying to locate his parental family:

- *Imprecise origin.* Several records point to a Virginia birthplace for Vincent, but
none specifies a county or other locality.
- *Common surname.* The U.S. Census Bureau reported that Taylor was the tenth
most common surname in the United States in 1990.[3] It probably was at least
that common in early nineteenth-century Virginia.
- *Burned records.* When Vincent's county of origin was located with reasonable

---

[1]   "Scattered Pieces: Assembling a Family from Scanty Records," *The National Genealogical Society
Quarterly*, Vol 91, #3, September 2003, pp 183-195.

[2]   Suzanne Smith Ray, Lyndon H. Hart III, and J. Christian Kolbe, comps., "Introduction," *A Preliminary
Guide to Pre-1904 County Records in the Virginia State Library and Archives* (Richmond: Virginia State Library
and Archives, 1994), xii. Today the Virginia State Library and Archives is called the Library of Virginia.

[3]   "Frequently Occurring First Names and Surnames from the 1990 Census," U.S. Census Bureau, Population
Division, online at <www.census.gov/genealogy/names/dist.all.last>.

certainty, it turned out to be King and Queen County, one of the 20 percent of Virginia counties that had lost all of their early courthouse records.[4]

When research on Vincent Taylor began, he was known to be a Missouri citizen with origins somewhere in Virginia. After the case was built, he was placed securely in a reconstructed parental family in a specific community. The research leading to this outcome demonstrates resources and reasoning that many genealogists can use to locate ancestors despite destroyed courthouse records.

Vincent Taylor in Missouri

Vincent Taylor appeared in Warren County, Missouri, by January 1836, when he purchased a lot in Warrenton, the county seat.[5] He apparently lived out his life there. In May 1865, his widow petitioned the Warren County court to administer his estate and named his surviving children as heirs – Fountain Taylor, Katy Briscoe, Eli Taylor, Bernard Taylor, and Miranda Morris.[6]

Few Missouri records contain information related to Vincent's origins. Together the 1850 and 1860 censuses show that he was born in Virginia between 1797 and 1799.[7] Judging from the 1850 census, his youngest child was born in Virginia, 1832-33, so Vincent probably migrated between that time and his January 1836 appearance in Missouri. Another of Vincent's sons, in a late-in-life marriage record, named his parents as Vinson Taylor and Sarah Derm (possibly a phonetic spelling of Durham).[8]

Vincent's daughter, "Katy," married in Warren County, Missouri.[9] Her descendants possess a sampler that she stitched, probably while still living in Virginia. The sampler provides her birthdate as 13 January 1820, refers to her as "Kitty" and "Kiturrah" Taylor, and

---

[4]   The circumstances surrounding this disaster are described in Rev. Alfred Bagby, *King and Queen County, Virginia* (1908; reprint, Baltimore, Md.: Clearfield, 1990), 134; and Fred C. Ainsworth and Joseph W. Kirkley, *The War of the Rebellion: A Compilation of the Official Records of the Union and Confederate Armies,* series 1, 53 vols. (Washington D.C.: Government Printing Office, 1891), 33: 240-46.

[5]   *History of St. Charles, Montgomery, and Warren Counties, Missouri* (1885; reprint, St. Louis: Paul V. Cochrane, 1969), 1068. Lots in Warrenton were sold beginning in January 1836 to finance building a courthouse. The extant land records of Warren Co., however, do not begin until 1838.

[6]   Warren Co. Will Book C: 469, Probate Court, Warrenton, Mo.; microfilm 0,067,401, Family :History Library (FHL), Salt Lake City, Utah. Prior to locating this petition naming Vincent's children directly, the present author built a case from indirect and negative evidence to show that Miranda Taylor was Vincent's daughter. See William M. Litchman, "Widows, Stepkin, and Support Networks: Clues to the Unknown Father of Miranda (Taylor) Morris," *NGS Quarterly* 84 (March 1996): 17-27.

[7]   Vincent Taylor household, 1850 U.S. Census, Warren Co., Mo., pop. sch., dist. 99, p. 40, dwell. 189, fam. 199; National Archives (NA) microfilm publication M432, roll 421. Also, Vincent Taylor household, 1860 U.S. Census, Warren Co., Mo., pop. sch., Elkhorn twp., Warrenton post office, p. 10, dwell./fam. 61;l NA microfilm M653, roll 659.

[8]   Eli Patterson Taylor and Elisebeth Nancy Perrin marriage, 14 April 1897, Wisconsin Marriages, Grant Co., 1893-97, vol. 8, p. 95, Bureau of Vital Statistics, Madison, Wisc.; FHL microfilm 1,266,663.

[9]   William Brisco and Catherine Taylor marriage, 18 March 1843, Warren Co. Marriage Record A: 91, Recorder of Deeds, Warrenton, Mo., FHL microfilm 0,967,394.

includes the initials of her parents and siblings. It also has a puzzling notation – "Maly Watts John Watts bo April 1830" – that proved to be a clue to her father's parental family.[10]

Locating Vincent's probable place of origin

Because Vincent Taylor moved from Virginia to Missouri apparently in the 1830s, research turned to locating him in Virginia's 1830 census. Only two Vincent Taylor households were found in the state that year, one in Fauquier County and the other in King and Queen County.[11] Two factors rule out the Fauquier County Vincent as the Vincent who settled in Missouri by January 1836:

> o The 1830 configuration of the Fauquier County household is incompatible with what is known of the Missouri Vincent's family. (For example, the only adult male in the Fauquier County household is in his fifties in 1830, when the Missouri Vincent would have been in his early thirties.)
> o The Fauquier County Vincent was enumerated there in the 1840 census, while the Vincent in question was living in Missouri.[12]

In addition, unlike the Fauquier County Vincent, the age range indicated for the Vincent Taylor in King and Queen County in 1830 and the ages of his apparent wife and children are consistent with the configuration of the Vincent Taylor household in the 1840 census of Warren County, Missouri.

Listed on the line below Vincent Taylor in the 1830 census of King and Queen County is Caleb Taylor.[13] Although Caleb was not named in King and Queen County's 1840 census, he appeared there in 1810 and 1820.[14] The three censuses in which he was found are correlated in table 1. The correlation shows that Caleb was born in 1760-65 and that his apparent wife was born 1770-75. Both were of an appropriate age to have been the parents of Vincent, who was born 1797-99. As shown in table 1, the Caleb Taylor household included a male of Vincent's age in 1810 but not in 1820. The Missouri Vincent, however, was married and had two children in 1820 so would not necessarily have been enumerated

[10]   The sampler is in the care of Barbara Lewellen; 6485 Ace Court; Longmont, CO 80503-8330. Photographs are in possession of the author. An image of the sampler can be seen online at <freepages.genealogy.rootsweb.com/~bldr/realabc.html>. The reconstruction of Caleb Taylor's family on Ms. Lewellen's web site is based on an early version prepared by the present author.

[11]   Voincent Taylor household, 1830 U.S. Census, Fauquier Co., Va., p. 454, line 26; NA microfilm M19, roll 194. Also, Vincent Taylor household, 1830 U.S. Census, King and Queen Co., Va., p. 289, line 24; NA microfilm M19, roll 201.

[12]   Vincent Taylor household, 1840 U.S. Census, Warren Co., Mo., Hickory Grove twp., p. 170, line 16, NA microfilm M704, roll 233.

[13]   Caleb Taylor household, 1830 U.S. Census, King and Queen Co., Va., p. 289, line 25; NA microfilm M19, roll 201.

[14]   Caleb Taylor household, 1810 U.S. Census, King and Queen Co., Val, p. 227, line 7; NA microfilm M252, roll 69. Also, Caleb Taylor household, 1820 U.S. Census, King and Queen Co., Va., p. 187/214, line 16; NA microfilm M33, roll 142, frame 29.

60

in a parental household. (Unfortunately, he has not been located in the 1820 census.)

The census information is compelling. It alone is not sufficient, however, for researchers to conclude that Vincent was a son of Caleb Taylor. Reconstructing Caleb's family, however, should clarify whether Vincent fits into his family or not.

Building the case for Vincent's parental family

Table 1 shows that the 1810-30 censuses imply that Caleb Taylor had six sons and three daughters. The fact that Caleb was not enumerated in King and Queen County in 1840 suggests that he could have died there in the 1830s. With such a possibility, researchers would be likely to consult probate records to verify Caleb's death and to identify his children. The burning of the King and Queen County courthouse in 1864, however, would have destroyed all of its records of Caleb's estate and heirs. Reconstructing a family in such circumstances presents special challenges. Researchers must collect pieces of information from scattered sources and integrate them to re-assemble an ancestral family. The many sources of information that genealogists might be able to locate and use for this purpose include the following:

o *Surviving or reconstructed county records.* Counties suffering heavy record losses sometimes made an effort to reconstruct their destroyed records. After King and Queen County's disastrous fire, for example, the county assigned a committee of processioners to describe the boundaries of all land holdings in the county.[15]

o *State-level records.* Records created by or submitted to the state often contain information on individual citizens. Sometimes this information is sufficient to help genealogists reconstruct ancestral families in burned-record counties. Examples include petitions to the governor or legislature, state censuses, state militia rolls or state copies of local militia rolls, local lawsuits appealed to state or district courts, and state copies of county vital records or tax lists.

o *Federal records.* Records created by the U.S. government are well known to genealogists and can be of great value when researching families in burned counties. These include federal censuses, land and tax records, local cases heard in federal courts (bankruptcies, for example), and sources related to military service.

o *Records of non-governmental entities.* Several bodies in most counties created records of individual citizens separate from official county records. These include churches, cemeteries, newspapers, and schools. Their records might be found in the hands of their successors at the local level today, or could be in an archive or historical society, perhaps distant from where the records were created.

o *Records in private hands.* Often found in state or local historical societies or

---

15   Processioner's Report Book, 1867-68, Clerk of the Circuit Court, King and Queen Co., King and Queen Courthouse, Va.; FHL microfilm 1,986,827, item 2.

archives, private records can include diaries, family Bibles, letters, merchants' accounts, midwives' and undertakers' notes, ministers' records, and other sources of information on individuals and families in counties with burned courthouse records. Like records of non-governmental entities, material in private hands might be located today far from the county where it was created.

o *Later county records.* Even though a courthouse fire may have destroyed all of the records made during an ancestor's lifetime, descendants, relatives, or neighbors many years later may have created county records containing information about the long-deceased ancestor.

Even though many resources may be available to researchers after a courthouse has burned, records pertinent to a particular family still may be scarce. The scattered items relevant to Caleb Taylor's family are perhaps typical. A few of the record types mentioned above provided useful information, but most did not. The most helpful were tax lists, federal censuses, state copies of vital records, church minutes and membership rolls, and the hand-stitched sampler mentioned previously, found in private hands.

State copy of tax lists

Tax lists are perhaps the most valuable resource for genealogical research in Virginia's burned counties. Virginia has collected taxes annually since 1782 except for 1808 when the state failed to provide for taxation. Historically, Virginia's tax commissioners were local officials, but they sent lists of taxpayers to the state each year. Consequently, tax records are available to researchers for most years and most Virginia counties, whether the courthouse burned or not. The lists consist of two series:

o *Land tax lists*, which show the name of each landowner, acreage, and tax. As the years progressed the information in the lists increased, including distance and direction from the courthouse, neighbors' names, and basis for the assessment. Virginia's land tax lists often include notations or appendices (sometimes called "alterations") showing how a taxpayer acquired or disposed of a particular tract of land.

o *Personal property tax lists*, which generally show the name of every male over the age of sixteen or twenty-one (depending on the tax year), except for the aged and infirm, and the basis for the tax. In the early years, taxable personal property was limited to livestock and slaves, but in later years various household and farm items also were taxed.[16]

---

[16]   For further information about Virginia's land and personal property tax records, see Conley L. Edwards, comp., "Using Land Tax Records in the Archives at the Library of Virginia (Research Notes Number 1)," online at <www.lva.lib.va.us/whatwehave/tax/m3_persprop.htm>.

Table 1

**Correlation of 1810-30 Censuses for Caleb Taylor Household
King and Queen County, Virginia**

1810	1820	1830	Correlation and Suggested Identity
	male 0-10 (b. 1810-20)	male 15-19 (b. 1810-14)	son, b. 1810-15
male 0-10 (b. 1800-10)	male 10-15 (b. 1804-10)	male 20-29 (b. 1800-10)	son, b. 1804-10
male 0-10 (b. 1800-10)			son, b. 1800-10
male 10-15 (b. 1794-1800)			son, b. 1794-1800
male 10-15 (b. 1794-1800)			son, b. 1794-1800
male 26-44 (b. 1765-84)	male over 45 (b. 1775 or bef)	male 60-69 (b. 1760-70)	Caleb Taylor b. 1760-65
		female 0-5 (b. 1825-30)	unknown
	female 0-10 (b. 1810-20)	female 15-19 (b. 1810-15)	daughter, b. 1810-15
female 0-10 (b. 1800-10)	female 16-25 (b. 1794-1804)	female 20-29 (b. 1800-10)	daughter, b. 1800-04
female 0-10 (b. 1800-10)			daughter, b. 1800-10
female 26-44 (b. 1765-84)	female over 45 (b. 1775 or bef)	female 50-59 (b. 1770-80)	Caleb Taylor's wife b. 1770-75
female 26-44 (b. 1765-84)			unknown

Note: censuses are cited in the text.

In addition to providing information about Caleb Taylor's land, King and Queen County's land tax lists contain sufficient information to identify his widow and three of his children. Caleb paid taxes continuously from 1813 to 1839 on 54 3/4 acres of land located five miles north of the King and Queen County courthouse that he had purchased from "Ro." Thurston.[17] The "persons adjoining" were John Watts in 1814-19, John Watts estate in 1820, James Hart in 1821-23, and James Hart estate in 1824-39. In 1840-41, this property was listed as "Taylor, Caleb, Estate."[18] In 1842, two listings replaced it. One was a fee simple listing for 43 acres under the name of Francis Prince (four miles north of the court house).[19] The other was a life estate of 11 3/4 acres (five miles north) under the names of Mary Ann and Frances Taylor.[20] Both entries include explanatory notes. The Prince note states "transferred from Caleb Taylor's Estate by deed from Nancy Taylor, admx." The Taylor note reads: "Under the will of Caleb Taylor, decd, (and) 43 acres transferred to Francis Prince by deed from Nancy Taylor, admx of Caleb Taylor, decd."

The above notes apparently refer to a deed and other legal actions recorded in the King and Queen County courthouse before its destruction. The 1842 Taylor note mentions Caleb's will but calls Nancy an administratrix. Either Caleb failed to name an executor in his will or the person he designated was unable or unwilling to fill that role. As a result, the court appointed Nancy to administer the estate. Because it is unlikely that a female other than a widow would have been given that responsibility, Nancy Taylor probably was Caleb's widow. In addition, Mary Ann and Frances Taylor, to whom Caleb apparently bequeathed a life interest in about one-fifth of his land, probably were his children.

From 1845 through 1854 the land tax books include entries for Nancy Taylor's payment of taxes on 44½ acres thirty miles northwest of the King and Queen Courthouse that she had purchased from John B. Martin.[21] An 1855 listing for the same acreage under the

[17] Caleb Tayulor entry, 1813 land tax list, Benjamin Faulkner's dist., p. 12, King and Queen Co., Va; 1814, John W. Fleet's dist. Unpaginated; 1815, Francis Rowe's dist., p. 18; 1816, Francis Row's dist., unpaginated, 1817, Francis Row's dist., p. 20; 1818, Francis Row's dist., p. 20; 1819, Francis Row's dist., p. 20; 1820, Francis Row's dist., p. 23; 1821, Ro. Courtney's dist., p. 28; 1822, Robert Courtney's dist., p. 26; 1823, Francis Row's dist., p. 28; 1824, Francis Row's dist., p. 25; 1825, Francis Row's dist., p. 24; 1826, Francis Row's dist., p. 26; 1827, John Pollard's dist., unpaginated; 1828, John Pollard's dist., p. 28; 1829, John Pollard's dist., p. 28; 1830, John Pollard's dist., p. 26; 1831, John Pollard's dist., p. 31; 1832, John Pollard's dist., p. 28; 1833, John Pollard's dist., p. 28; 1834, John Pollard's dist., p. 28; 1835, Parmenas Bird's dist., p. 32; 1836 Parmenas Bird's dist., p. 30; 1837, Parmenas Bird's dist., p. 30; 1838, John Pollard's dist., p. 32; and 1839, John Pollard's dist., p. 32. See King and Queen Co., Va., Land Tax Lists, 1782-1818, Library of Virginia, Richmond; FHL microfilm 0,029,941. Also, 1819-44; FHL microfilm 0,029,942.

[18] Caleb Taylor estate entry, 1840 land tax list, John Pollard's dist., p. 31, King and Queen Co., Va; and 1841, John Pollard's dist., unpaginated.

[19] Francis Prince entry, 1842 land tax list, John Pollard's dist., p. 25, King and Queen Co., Va.

[20] Mary Ann and Frances Taylor entry, 1842 land tax list, John Pollard's dist., p. 31, King and Queen Co., Va.

[21] Nancy Taylor entry, 1845 land tax list, John Pollard's dist., p. 25, King and Queen Co., Va; 1846, John Pollard's dist., p. 30; 1847, John Pollard's dist., p. 31; 1848, John Pollard's dist., p. 30; 1849, John Pollard's dist., p. 29; 1850, John Pollard's disst., p. 30; 1851, James A. Golden's dist., p. 31; 1852, James A. Golden's dist., p. 30; 1853, John H. Watkins's dist., p. 30; and 1854, John H. Watkins's dist., p. 30. See King and Queen Co., Va., Land Tax Lists, 1845-63, Library of Virginia; FHL microfilm 0,029,943.

64

name of Philip Taylor contains the note, "by death of Mother."[22] As Nancy's adult son, Philip apparently was Caleb's son as well.

Like the land tax lists, the personal property tax lists also aid in identifying members of Caleb Taylor's family. Caleb first paid personal property taxes in Essex County, Virginia, 1801-02,[23] then in King and Queen county continuously 1804-39.[24] From 1801 to 1812, the only taxable white male in the Caleb Taylor household was over age sixteen – undoubtedly Caleb himself. In 1813 the number rose to two, which could imply that one of Caleb's sons turned sixteen in 1812 and was born in 1796. In 1815, the number of taxable males rose to three, implying a son born in 1799.

From 1816 to 1817, Caleb's taxable white males decreased by one. In 1817, two Taylors – George and Carter – made their first appearance in the King and Queen County tax list.[25] Because Carter was listed in a different district from Caleb Taylor, and because Carter had paid taxes in 1816 in Essex County, he probably does not account for the decrease in the number of taxable males in Caleb's household.[26] In contrast, George Taylor paid taxes only after the decrease in the number of taxable males in Caleb's household, and every time George paid taxes in King and Queen County (1817-20) he was listed next to Caleb – which might or might not indicate that they lived near each other.[27] In any case, the personal property tax lists provide indirect evidence suggesting that George was Caleb's eldest son.

Between 1818 and 1819 the number of taxable males in Caleb Taylor's household again decreased by one. The only Taylor newly appearing in the King and Queen County tax list in 1819 was Vincent Taylor.[28] Altogether, Vincent paid personal property taxes eight

----

[22]   Philip Taylor entry, 1855 land tax list, John H. Watkins's dist., p. 30, King and Queen Co., Va.

[23]   Caleb Taylor entry, 1801 personal property tax list, p. 14; and 1802, p. 15; Essex Co., Va., Personal Property Tax Lists, 1782-1818, Library of Virginia; FHL micofilm 2,024,527.

[24]   Caleb Taylor entry, 1804 personal property tax list, Benjamin Shackelford's dist., p. 13, King and Queen Co., Va.; 1805, Thomas Spencer's dist., p. 11; 1806, Thomas Spencer's dist., p. 13; 1807, Thomas Spencer's dist., p. 11; 1809, Benjamin Faulkner's dist., p. 11; 1810, Benjamin Faulkner's dist., p. 15; 1811, Benjamin Faulkner's dist., p. 16; 1812, Benjamin Faulkner's dist., p. 13; 1813, Benjamin Faulkner's dist., p. 13, King and Queen Co., Va; 1814, John W. Fleet's dist. p. 15; 1815, Francis Rowe's dist., p. 13; 1816, Francis Row's dist., p. 14, 1817, Francis Row's dist., p. 14; 1818, Francis Row's dist., p. 15; 1819, Robert Courtney's dist., p. 15; 1820, Francis Row's dist., p. 15; 1821, R. Courtney's dist., p. 1928; 1822, Robert Courtney's dist., p. 26; 1823, Francis Row's dist., p. 29; 1824, Francis Row's dist., p. 27; 1825, Harris Carleton's dist., unpaginated; 1826, Harris Carleton's dist., p. 23; 1827, John Pollard's dist., p. 21; 1828, John Pollard's dist., p. 20; 1829, John Pollard's dist., p. 20; 1830, John Pollard's dist., p. 19; 1831, John Pollard's dist., p. 22; 1832, John Pollard's dist., p. 23; 1833, John Pollard's dist., p. 21; 1834, John Pollard's dist., p. 21; 1835, Parmenas Bird's dist., p. 24; 1836 Parmenas Bird's dist., p. 26; 1837, Parmenas Bird's dist., p. 25; 1838, John Pollard's dist., p. 22; and 1839, John Pollard's dist., p. 22. See King and Queen Co., Va., Personal Propetry Tax Lists, 1804-23, FHL microfilm 0,032,121. Also, 1824-46; FHL microfilm 0,032,122.

[25]   Carter Taylor entry, 1817 personal property tax list, Robert Courtney's dist., p. 14; and George Taylor entry, 1817 personal property tax list, Francis Row's dist., p. 14; King and Queen Co., Va., Personal Property Tax Lists.

[26]   Carter Taylor entry, 1816 personal property tax list, p. 16, Essex Co., Va., Personal Property Tax Lists.

[27]   George Taylor entry, 1817 personal property tax list, Francis Row's dist., p. 14; 1818, Francis Row's dist., p. 15; 1819, Robert Courtney's dist., p 15; King and Queen Co., Va., Personal Property Tax Lists.

[28]   Vincent Taylor entry, 1819 personal property tax list, Robert Coutney's dist., p. 14, King and Queen Co, Va., Personal Property Tax Lists.

times in King and Queen County: 1819-20, 1823-25, 1831, and 1834-35.[29] Except for 1819-20, both Vincent and Caleb paid taxes in the same district. In 1823, 1831, and 1834, their names are contiguous – which again might or might not indicate that they lived near each other. Nonetheless, the information from the personal property tax lists supports the possibility that Caleb Taylor was Vincent Taylor's father.

Between them, King and Queen County's land and personal property tax lists appear to identify Caleb Taylor's widow (Nancy), three of his sons (George, Philip, and Vincent) and two of his daughters (Frances and Mary Ann). Further research in King and Queen County tax lists, censuses, church records, and a reconstructed plat book produced seemingly random information on dozens of people named Taylor. The tentative identification of Caleb Taylor's widow and five children from the tax lists, however, enabled selecting information related to Caleb's family and using it to identify additional children.

State copy of vital records

A wide-ranging search of vital records turned up direct evidence of one of Caleb Taylor's sons. When he married his second or third wife in 1866, Lewis Taylor of King and Queen County reported that Caleb was his father.[30] Lewis also reported that his mother was "Ann Durham." Because Nancy is a common nickname for Ann, Lewis almost certainly provided the maiden name of "Nancy Taylor," who the land tax notations implied was Caleb's widow.

The information that Lewis was a son of Caleb Taylor prompted a review of Lewis's tax listings. Lewis's first land tax listing, in 1828, noted that his land was held "in right of wife who was Nancy Durham."[31] In 1861-63, Lewis paid personal property taxes for a second taxable male. In 1861 that person was captioned "nephew," in 1862 he was "boy Joshua over 19," and in 1863, he was "Joshua Taylor age 20."[32] In the 1860 census, Joshua Taylor, age seventeen, was enumerated in Lewis's household.[33] In 1850, however, Joshua was an eight-year-old in the Brooking Taylor household in King and Queen County, appearing to be Brooking's son.[34] Because Joshua Taylor appears to have been both nephew of Lewis Taylor and son of Brooking Taylor, Lewis and Brooking probably were brothers. Thus, Brooking Taylor apparently was another son of Caleb Taylor.

[29]   Ibid. Also, Vincent Taylor entry, 1820 personal property tax list, Francis Row's dist., p. 15; 1823, Francis Row's dist., p. 29; 1824, Francis Row's dist., p. 27; 1825, Harris Carleton's dist., unpaginated, 1831, John Pollard's dist.., p. 22; 1834, John Pollard's dist., p. 21; and 1835, Parmenas Bird's dist., p. 24; King and Queen Co., Va., Personal Property Tax Lists.

[30]   Lewis Taylor and Martha I. Broach marriage, 25 December 1866, Essex Co. Marriages 1853-1911, p. 89, line 48, Bureau of Vital Statistics, Richmond, Va.; Library of Virginia microfilm 15.

[31]   Lewis Taylor entry, 1828 land tax list, John Pollard's dist., p. 29, King and Queen Co. Land Tax Lists.

[32]   Lews Taylor entry, 1861 personal property tax list, Thomas R. Gresham's dist., p. 37; 1862,m p. 41; 1863, p. 41; King and Queen Co., Va., Personal Property Tax Lists, 1860-63; FHL microfilm 0,032,125.

[33]   Lewis Taylor household, 1860 U.S. census, King and Queen Co., Va., pop. sch., Stevensville post office, p. 425, dwell./fam. 3; NA microfilm M653, roll 1357.

[34]   Brooking Taylor household, 1850 U.S. census, King and Queen Co., Va., pop. sch., Drysdale Par., p. 203, dwell. 894, fam. 891; NA microfilm M432, roll 954.

The vital records search also revealed the connection between Caleb Taylor and Francis Prince, the grantee who obtained most of Caleb's land. Catherine and Milton Prince, a brother and sister who married on the same day in 1875, reported that their parents were Francis Prince and Frances Taylor.[35] Caleb's land was not sold out of the family, because Francis Prince appears to have been his son-in-law. In addition, Milton's bride was alice B. Taylor, whose reported father was Brooking Taylor. Theirs apparently was a first-cousin marriage – not unusual in this time and place – because both Frances (née Taylor) Prince and Brooking Taylor probably were children of Caleb Taylor.

Federal censuses

Caleb Taylor's probable widow and five children, identified above, were enumerated in the 1850 census of King and Queen County, as follows:

o Nancy Taylor, age 70, living in the household of Philip Taylor in Drysdale Parish;[36]

o Mary Ann Taylor, age 50, living in the household of Francis Prince in St. Stephen's Parish;[37]

o Lewis Taylor, age 43, living in St. Stephens Parish;[38]

o Frances Prince, age 39, also living in the household of Francis Prince, her apparent husband;[39]

o Brooking Taylor, age 36, living in Drysdale Parish;[40]

o Philip Taylor, age 35.[41]

Enumerated six households after the household containing Francis and Frances Prince and Mary Ann Taylor was James Taylor, age 41.[42] His age and location in the census suggest that James was another of Caleb Taylor's sons. In addition, James's occupation was carpenter – the same occupation reported for Brooking Taylor in 1850 and Lewis Taylor in 1860.[43] Also, a child in James's household bore the same name as one of Caleb Taylor's

[35]   Marriages of J. F. Crowe to Catharine A. Prince and Milton C. Prince to Allice B. Taylor, 21 April 1875, King and Queen Co., Register of Marriages 1: 15, nos. 35-36, County Clerk, King and Queen Courthouse, Va.,; FHL microfilm 1,986,828.

[36]   Philip Taylor household, 1850 U.S. census, King and Queen Co., Va., pop. sch., Drysdale Par., p. 199, dwell./fam. 827; NA microfilm M432, roll 954.

[37]   Francis Prince household, 1850 U.S. census, King and Queen Co., Va., pop. sch., St. Stephens Par., p. 149, dwell./fam. 2; NA microfilm M432, roll 954.

[38]   Lewis Taylor houshold, 1850 U.S. census, King and Queen Co., Va., pop. sch., St. Stephens Par., p. 155, dwell./fam. 107; NA microfilm M432, roll 954.

[39]   1850 U.S. census, King and Queen Co., Va., pop. sch., St. Stephens Par., p. 149, dwell./fam. 2.

[40]   1850 U.S. census, King and Queen Co., Va., pop. sch., Drysdale Par., p. 203, dwell. 894, fam. 891.

[41]   1850 U.S. census, King and Queen Co., Va., pop. sch., Drysdale Par., p. 199, dwell/fam. 827.

[42]   James Taylor houshold, 1850 U.S. census, King and Queen Co., Va., pop. sch., St. Stephens Par., p. 149, dwell./fam. 7; NA microfilm M432, roll 954.

[43]   1860 U.S. census, King and Queen Co., Va., pop. sch., Stevensville post office, p. 425, dwell./fam. 3.

known sons, Philip Taylor.

Church records

Membership lists and minutes of the Mattaponi Baptist Church in King and Queen County name several individuals who appear to have been members of Caleb Taylor's family in the 1830s through the 1850s. They were Frances A. Prince and her husband, Francis Prince, Brooking Taylor, James Taylor, and Lewis Taylor.[44] In addition, an 1832 membership list includes "Mrs. Taylor, wife of Vincent."[45] Minutes dated September 1835 report that "sister Taylor who is about to remove to the west is dismissed from this church, and it is ordered that the clerk give her a letter of dismission recommending her to the communion of some sister church."[46] In isolation, these references – which do not mention relationships – appear to have little genealogical value. Nevertheless when considered in the context of the information from the other sources concerning Caleb Taylor's family, membership in the same church supports the conclusion that the Princes and Brooking, James, Lewis, and Vincent Taylor were members of one family.

Assembling Caleb Taylor's family

As noted previously, table 1 provides a composite of the 1810-30 census entries for Caleb Taylor's household implying that Caleb had six sons and three daughters. Tax records identified Caleb's widow as Nancy Taylor. She headed a household in the 1840 census of King and Queen County, but that enumeration does not add to or conflict with the 1810-30 census information implying that Caleb Taylor had nine children.[47] The non-courthouse sources described above identify two of these children directly. These records identify six additional children indirectly, although the degree of certainty varies. Table 2 summarizes those results.

Placing Vincent Taylor in Caleb Taylor's family

No record states that Caleb Taylor of King and Queen County, Virginia, was the father of Virginia-born Vincent Taylor of Warren County, Missouri. Nevertheless, the evidence strongly supports this conclusion. Specific points include the following:

o The maiden name of Vincent Taylor's wife was reported to be "Derm,"

[44] W. T. Hundley, *History of Mattaponi Baptist Church, King and Queen County, Virginia* (Richmond Appeals Press, 1928); FHL microfilm 1,425,567. See pp. 170, 207, 509, and 514 for Frances Prince; 116, 121, 191, 207, 249, 252, and 509 for Francis Prince; 116, 118, and 121 for Brooking Taylor; 117, 195, and 265 for James Taylor; and 365 for Lewis Taylor.

[45] Ibid., 117.

[46] Ibid., 133.

[47] Nancy Taylor household, 1840 U.S. census, King and Queen Co., Va., p. 102, line 7; NA microfilm M704, roll 564.

probably a phonetic spelling of Durham. Both Caleb Taylor and one of his sons, Lewis, married women whose maiden name was Durham.

o Two Vincent Taylors headed households in the 1830 census of Virginia, one in Fauquier County and the other in King and Queen County. The Vincent in Fauquier County can be ruled out as having settled in Missouri by 1836. The enumeration of Vincent Taylor in King and Queen County immediately precedes that of Caleb Taylor,

o Vincent Taylor of Missouri was born 1797-99. In Virginia, he would have become a sixteen-year-old taxable male 1813-15. Caleb Taylor began paying taxes for an additional taxable male in 1815.

o Vincent Taylor began paying taxes under his own name in 1819, the same year that the number of taxable males reported by Caleb Taylor decreased by one. This was about the time that the Missouri Vincent Taylor would have become twenty-one years old.

o In six of the eight years that Vincent Taylor paid taxes in King and Queen County, he was listed in the same tax district as Caleb Taylor.

o Vincent Taylor's wife was a member of the Mattaponi Baptist Church in King and Queen County in 1832. Brooking Taylor, James Taylor, and Frances Prince, children of Caleb Taylor, belonged to the same church. Their brother, Lewis Taylor, was associated with the church.

o Vincent Taylor left Virginia between 1832-33 when his youngest son was born there and January 1836 when he purchased land in Missouri. Vincent's wife very likely was the "sister Taylor" to whom the Mattaponi Baptist Church granted a letter of dismissal in 1835, when she was "about to remove to remove to the west."

o King and Queen County tax records show that John Watts was a neighbor of Caleb Taylor. A sample created by a daughter of Vincent Taylor, probably while still living in Virginia, contains the name "John Watts."

Conclusion

Even where large groups of records are destroyed, researchers often can locate and assemble small scraps of evidence. By carefully studying the composite, they sometimes can place an ancestor into a parental family. In this way, the evidence presented here shows that the most likely father of Vincent Taylor was Caleb Taylor and that Vincent's mother may have been Caleb's widow, Ann or Nancy (née Durham) Taylor. This result relies on princples that authors have demonstrated in this journal many times:

o Leave no record unexamined. Even in locales with many missing records, gaps can be filled by bits that remain or have been reconstructed, including state and federal records and non-governmental sources like churches.

o Take advantage of whatever evidence can be found to reconstruct potential parental families for the starting-point ancestor. Use all of the identifying information – not just the ancestor's name – to match the ancestor to the most likely parental family.

o Focus on family groups and potential family members, not isolated individuals. Locate and analyze all of the records for each person in these groups, including every record of their property and any related documents.

o Build a convincing case supporting the likely parental relationship. To be credible, the research and the resulting case should address the five elements of the standard of proof for genealogy: a reasonably exhaustive search for information concerning the relationship in question, complete and accurate citations of each source used, analysis of the collected information to determine its value as evidence of the relationship; resolution of any conflicting evidence; and a soundly reasoned conclusion.[48]

The challenge of narrowing a migrating ancestor's point of origin to at least the county level can frustrate genealogists, especially if common surnames like Taylor are involved. When researchers find the county and learn that its record losses are significant, they may admit defeat and never discover the treasure that may remain. Vincent Taylor's parental family demonstrates, however, that frustration and surrender may be unnecessary. Even when records are scarce, confidently identifying and reconstructing an ancestral family is possible.

---

[48]   Board for Certification of Genealogists, *The BCG Genealogical Standards Manual* (Orem, Utah, Ancestry, 2000), 1-2.

Table 2

Suggested Identities of Caleb Taylor's Children Implied by 1810-30 Censuses and Other King and Queen County, Virginia, Sources

Identities Suggested by 1810-30 Censuses	Identities Suggested by Other Sources	Sources Indicating Suggested Identities
son, b. 1810-15	Philip Taylor, b. 1814-15	land tax lists
son, b. 1810-20	Brooking Taylor, b. 1813-14	personal property tax lists census, church records
son, b. 1804-10	James Taylor, b. 1808-09	census, church records
son, b 1800-10	Lewis Taylor, b 1806-07	census, church records
son, b. 1794-1800	Vincent Taylor, b 1797-98	personal property tax lists church records
son, b. 1794-1800	George Taylor	personal property tax lists
daughter, b. 1810-15	Frances Taylor, b. 1810-11; m. Francis Prince	land tax lists, vital records, census
daughter, b. 1800-04	unknown	
daughter, b. 1800-10	Mary Ann Taylor, b. 1799-1800	land tax lists, census

Notes: Suggested identities in the first column are based on figure 1. Birthdates in the second column are calculated from entries in the 1850 census, cited in the text.

Chapter 9

Using Cluster Methodology to Backtrack an Ancestor:
The Case of John Bradberry[1]

> Perhaps the most common genealogical mistake is
> focusing a search too narrowly. Broadening research to
> include a cluster of migrating families can lead to
> convincing evidence of birthplace and parents.

Tracing a migrating ancestor's origin requires (1) targeting the correct location, (2) recognizing the person in its records, and (3) identifying the ancestor's parental family. Common complications, however, may block these goals:

o Records in the place of settlement might not specify origin, or they name a
   general jurisdiction unlikely to have records detailing parentage.
o Name, age, and state of birth may not be enough to identify a settler in a prior
   location, especially if the name is common.
o When a precise origin is determined, its records do not identify the migrating
   ancestor directly.

A11 three problems apply to John Bradberry a Virginia native who settled in Tennessee and Arkansas. Only censuses report his birthplace.[2] Bradberrys, including several Johns, appear in various Virginia counties. Which – if any – was the Tennessee-Arkansas settler?

Several strategies might lead to an answer, but cluster methodology is the most promising. Because people usually migrated in groups, or followed one another, neighbors

---

[1] _"Using Cluster Methodology to Backtrack an Ancestor: The Case of John Bradberry," *The National Genealogical Society Quarterly*, Vol 95, #3, June 2007, pp 103-116.

[2] _J. Bradberry household, 1850 U.S. census, Weakley Co., Tenn., pop. sch., Dist. 2, p. 468 (stamped, recto), dwell./fam. 37; National Archives (NA) microfilm M432, roll 899. In 1860 this J. Bradberry appears as John. See John Bradberry household, 1860 U.S. census, Greene Co., Ark., pop. sch., Concord twp., Oak Bluff post office, p. 112, dwell. 670, fam. 655; NA microfilm M653, roll 42. Also, J. N. Bradberry household, 1870 U.S. Census, Greene Co., Ark., pop. sch., Johnson twp., Big Creek post office, p. 8, dwell./fam. 52; NA microfilm M593, roll 54.

often came from the same place. Compared with focusing on one ancestor, studying neighborhood clusters yields more clues to ancestral origin and identity.

The Bradberry cluster

In 1850 John Bradberry lived in Weakley County, Tennessee, near other Bradberry men born in Virginia between 1800 and 1816. Their children's birthplaces suggest that the fathers – probably brothers or cousins – had left Virginia between 1834 and 1838. See table 1. A source of unknown reliability identifies the parents of one of them, Henry Bradberry, as "Richard and Ann," but does not state his relationship to the others.[3] Bradberrys do not appear in most Weakley County court records.[4] County deeds and tax rolls, however, suggest ties and additional kin among the 1850 Bradberry cluster.

The earliest Bradberry deed in Weakley County is dated 24 Ocrober 1823. Elizabeth Dickson of Carteret County, North Carolina, released her rights to 640 acres to James Bradberry of Wayne County, North Carolina.[5] On 12 November 1823 Samuel and Daniel Smith transferred an adjoining tract to Bradberry.[6] By 1834 Bradberry, settled in Perry county, Alabama, had sold the land.[7]

Weakley County deeds identify six Bradberrys, including John, living there between about 1837 and 1858:

o On 12 August 1837 James F, Bradberry pledged livestock, a rifle, tools, and household goods to secure $37.38 borrowed from James Etheridge. The deed mentions a note dated "first of October last" (1836).[8]

o In separate deeds between 1847 and 1855 Richard, Henry and Joseph Bradberry made or secured loans.[9]

o On 29 August 1847 Robert S. Bradberry purchased one hundred acres from

---

[3]   Henry Bradberry family Bible record, photocopy (in part) and transcription (in part) by Carolyn Wilcoxen (San Antonio, Tex.), publication data not available, in author's files.

[4]   Weakley Co. wills, 1828-1900, County Court, Dresden, Tenn.; microfilm 0,988,756, Family History Library (FHL), Salt Lake City. Weakley Co. inventories, County Court, Dresden, Tenn.; FHL microfilm 0,988,664. Weakley Co. guardians' settlements, 1843-66, County Court, Dresden, Tenn.; FHL microfilm 0,988,662. Weakley Co. marriages, 1843-66, County Court Clerk, Dresden, Tenn.; FHL microfilm 0,988,668.

[5]   Dickson to Bradberry, Weakley Co. Deed Book A: 328-29, Register of Deeds, Dresden, Tenn.,; FHL microfilm 0,988,760.

[6]   Smith and Smith to Bradbury, Weakley Co. Deed Book A:330-31.

[7]   Bradbury to Wade, power of attorney, Weakley Co. Deed Book A: 331. Bradbury to Blackmore, Weakley Co. Deed Book A: 370-71. Bradery to Smith, Weakley Co. Deed Book B: 73-74 and 76-77; FHL microfilm 0,988,760. Bradberry to Gardner, Weakley Co. Deed Book C: 397; FHL microfilm 0,988,761.

[8]   Bradbury to Etheridge, Weakley Co. Deed Book D: 412; FHL microfilm 0,988,761.

[9]   Trent to Richard Bradberry, Weakley Co. Deed Book H: 78; FHL microfilm 0,988,763. Henry Bradberry to Cochran, Weakley Co. Deed Book H: 318. Henry Bradberry to Trent, Weakley Co. Deed Book J: 197; FHL microfilm 0,988,764. Joseph Bradberry to White, Weakley Co. Deed Book J: 643. Joseph C. Bradberry to Cochran, Weakley Co. Deed Book M: 583-84; FHL microfilm 0,988,765.

Young P. Bowers.[10]

o On 8 October 1849 John Bradberry also purchased land from Young P. Bowers.[11] He sold it via a deed witnessed by Robert S. Bradberry on 12 October 1852.[12] On 1 November 1852 and 5 June 1854 John bought two more tracts from Bowers – acreage adjoining land owned or occupied by Richard and Robert "Bradberry." Robert Bradberry witnessed this deed as well.[13] After securing a debt on 4 August 1854, John sold his land on 3 November 1854.[14] John purchased another lot on 10 January 1858.[15] Finding himself in debt, he created a trust deed on 19 August 1858 and sold his land three months later.[16]

In Tennessee free white males age twenty-one through fifty paid annual poll taxes. The first payment, therefore, might indicate a birth twenty- one years earlier and the last a birth fifty years earlier. Many men, however, ignored or eluded the collectors.[17]

See Table 2 for Bradberry tax records in Weakley County.

The 1831-32 tax entries for James Bradberry pertain probably to the James who bought land in 1823, while living in North Carolina, and sold it in 1834, while living in Alabama. Conducting his Weakley County transactions through an attorney, he may have been a nonresident taxpayer. He has no known association with Virginia or the Bradberry cluster from Virginia. Moreover, born apparently in the 1770s, he was too old to be a sibling of any Weakley County Bradberry in 1850.[18]

Deeds identify the four household heads in the 1850 Bradberry cluster as Henry, John, Richard, and Robeft. A fifth associate, Joseph Bradberry who lived with "R." Bradberry in 1850, borrowed money in Weakley County in 1851 and 1855. The tax lists in table 2 suggest two more members of the cluster:

---

[10]   Bowers to Bradberry, Weakley Co. Deed Book H: 97.

[11]   Bowers to Bradbury Weakley Co. Deed Book K: 272-73; FHL microfilm 0,988,764.

[12]   Bradbury to Duke, Weakley Co. Deed Book K: 281-82.

[13]   Bowers to Bradbury, Weakley Co. Deed Book K: 301-2. Bowers to Bradberry, Weakley Co. Deed Book L: 617-18; FHL microfilm 0,988,765.

[14]   Bradberry to Bowers, Weakley Co. Deed Book M: 26. Bradberry to Gill, Weakley Co. Deed Book M: 182-83.

[15]   Finch to Bradberry, Weakley Co. Deed Book O: 431-32; FHL microfilm 0,988,766.

[16]   Bradberry to Drewry, Weakley Co. Deed Book P: 32-34; FHL microfilm 0,988,767. The deed mentions debt judgments against John. Also, Bradberry to Brasfield and others, Weakley Co. Deed Book P: 156-57.

[17]   Ann Evans Alley, "Taxation and Politics: Tennessee's Poll Tax Laws," *Middle Tennessee Journal of Genealogy and History* 11 (Fall 1997): 51-55. Also, Shirley Wilson, "An Introduction to Taxation for Genealogists," *Middle Tennessee Journal of Genealogy and History* 13 (Fall 1999): 51-57.

[18]   Jas Bradberry household, 1820 U.S. census, Wayne Co. N.C., p. 457, line 33; NA microfilm M33, roll 83. The household's oldest male was age forty-five or above. Also, James Bradberry household, 1830 U.S. census, Perry Co., Ala., p. 76, line 6; NA microfilm M19, roll 3. The household's oldest male was over age sixty and below age seventy.

74

Table 1

Bradberry Families in Weakley County, Tennessee, in 1850

DWELLING AND FAMILY	NAME	AGE	BIRTHPLACE
33	R. Bradberry	34	Virginia
	Elizabeth	22	Tennessee
	Isiah	3	Tennessee
	James	2	Tennessee
	Joseph	36	Virginia
	J. Ford	18	Tennessee
36	R. Bradberry	28	Virginia
	Elizabeth	30	Tennessee
	Ann	13	Tennessee
	George	9	Tennessee
	Richard	2	Tennessee
	A. J. Ford	13	Tennessee
37	J. Bradberry	40	Virginia
	Sarah	29	North Carolina
	George	4	Tennessee
42	H. Bradberry	50	Virginia
	Susan	34	Virginia
	Virginia	26	Virginia
	Elizabeth	24	Virginia
	Susan	22	Virginia
	James	21	Virginia
	Georgiann	18	Virginia
	John	16	Virginia
	Ann	15	Virginia
	Edmond	12	Tennessee
	William	8	Tennessee
	Gabrella	7	Tennessee
	Robert	6	Tennessee

Source: R. Bradberry, R. Bradberry, J. Bradberry, and H. Bradberry households, 1850 U.S. census, Weakley Co., Tenn., pop. sch. Dist. 7, p. 468 (stamped, recto and verso); National Archives microfilm M432, roll 899.

o James F. Bradberry paid taxes in the same district as John in 1847. He disappeared from Weakley County after 1846 and left no estate there. He does not appear in any 1850 census index.

o David Bradberry paid taxes in 1848-50 on one hundred acres but no deed identifies him as a grantee. On 29 August 1847, however, Robert S. Bradberry purchased one hundred acres for which he was never taxed. Robert apparently bought the land for David, which suggests a close relationship between them. David's appearance on the tax list in 1848 implies he was born in 1826-27.

These seven Bradberry men shared proximity, a Virginia birthplace, and socioeconomic status. Furthermore, John lived next to Richard, who associated with Robert, who associated with David. The birth range for the cluster from 1799-1800 (Henry) to 1826-77 (David) – means they could have been brothers. Additional research might verify or refute this possibility and locate John Bradberry's Virginia birthplace.

Montgomery County Bradberrys

The 1850 census suggests the Weakley County Bradberrys had moved from Virginia to Tennessee in the 1830s. Only two cluster members, however, headed Weakley County households in 1840.

o John Bradberry, whose household matches his family's composition in 1850
o James F Bradberry, who lived with five females perhaps next to John's home[19]

Where were the others from the 1850 cluster? Three Bradberry housholds in Montgomery County (three counties east of Weakley) – headed by H. L., Richard, and Mrs. A. Bradberry – seem to fill the gap. See Table 3.

Montgomery County deeds and a will show that the Bradberrys who paid taxes and voted there in the 1830s and early 1840s moved to Weakley County in the late 1840s:

o The earliest Bradberry deeds involved indebtedness – two for William in 1838 and one for Richard in 1840.[20]
o Henry and Joseph Bradberry secured debts between 1843 and 1846.[21]

---

[19]   Jno. Bradberry and Jas F Bradberry households, 1840 U.S. census, Weakley Co., Tenn., p. 292, lines 21-22; NA microfilm M704, roll 530. This enumeration is not alphabetized.

[20]   William Bradberry to Hampton, Montgomery Co. Deed Book P: 432, Register of Deeds, Clarksville, Tenn.; and William Bradberry to Edwards, Montgomery Co Deed Book R: 1; both on FHL microfilm 0,320,863. Richard Bradberry to Fanier, Montgomery Co. Deed Book S: 24; FHL microfilm 0,320,864.

[21]   Montgomery Co. Deed Book T: 284-85 (Henry Bradberry to Wade), 308 (Joseph Bradberry to Marr), 534 (Henry Bradberry to Johnson), and 584-85 (Joseph Bradberry to Johnson); FHL microfilm 0,320,865. Henry Bradberry to Waller, Montgomery Co. Deed Book W: 73 and 518; FHL microfilm 0,320,865.

Table 2

Bradberry Taxpayers in Weakley County, Tennessee, 1831-69

YEAR	GIVEN NAME	DISTRICT	TAXABLE ITEMS
1831-32	James		
1838	James E.	3	1 poll
1842	Jno.	3	1 poll
	James E.	3	1 poll
1843	John	3	1 poll
1844	John	8	1 poll
	James E.	14	1 poll
1845	James E.	14	1 poll
1846	John	7	1 poll
	James E.	14	1 poll
1847	John	7	1 poll
1848	John	7	1 poll
	David	7	1 poll, 100 acres, $150 value
1849	John	7	1 poll
	David	7	1 poll, 100 acres, $150 value
	Robert	7	1 poll, 100 acres, $200 value
1850	John	7	1 poll, 54 acres, $100 value
	David	7	1 poll, 100 acres, $150 value
	Robert S.	7	1 poll, 100 acres, $150 value
	Henry	7	1 poll
1851	Jno.	7	54 acres, $185 value
	Rob. S.	7	100 acres, $250 value
1858	John	7	103 acres
	Robt.	7	100 acres
	J. R.	7	
1859	R. S.	7	100 acres, $700 value
	J. R.	7	
	J. H.	7	
1860	J. H.	7	
1862	R. S.	7	100 acres, $600 value
	J. H.	7	100 acres, $600 value
1865	R. S.	7	
1866	R. S.	7	100 acres, $400 value
	E. T.	7	150 acres, $750 value
	William	7	
1868	J. H.	10	
	R. E.	7	

Sources: Weakley Co. 1828-32 tax lists, County Court, Dresden, Tenn.; microfilm 0,988,756, Family History Library (FHL), Salt Lake City. Also, Weakley Co. Tax Books 1-3, County Trustee, Dresden, Tenn.; FHL microfilm 1,003,115. Note: Lists before 1828 and for 1833-37, 1852-57, 1861, 1863-64, and 1867-68 are missing. No Bradberrys are listed in 1828-29. Some lists do not specify poll tax assessments, though a listing implies that the man owed or paid a poll tax. The search ended arbitrarily with 1869.

o On 26 January 1843 Robert S. and Ann Eliza Bradberry bought 87.5 acres from Samuel Wade. The deed's phrase "Robert S. Bradberry and Ann Eliza Bradberry, his & her heirs and assigns forever" implies that Ann Eliza was a feme sole, not a wife.[22]

o Ann Eliza Bradberry's will, dated 22 November 1843 and proved in February 1846, mentions her mother, Nancy Bradberry her brother Robert S. Bradberry, and George W. Bradberry. It refers to about forty-three acres on which "Robert S. Bradberry now lives."[23] The surname of witness Mary "Foard" appears twice within Weakley County Bradberry households in 1850.

o On 13 January 1846, probably soon after his sister Ann Eliza's death, Robert Bradberry sold part of the tract purchased from Samuel Wade.[24] On 3 July 1848 Robert, "of Weakley County," sold the remaining portion.[25]

Six Bradberrys – Henry, Joseph, Richard, William, and two Johns – paid Montgomery County taxes in 1836. Each, apparently between age twenty-one and fifty, lived in District 1 and owned no land or other taxable property.[26] Richard may have been the older of the two R. Bradberrys in Weakley County in 1850, because the younger, born in 1815-16, probably was not taxable in 1836. In 1841 Henry, Richard, and William Bradberry, over age twenty-one and living in District 2, were eligible to vote in Montgomery County.[27]

The cluster of Bradberrys surrounding John Bradberry lived in Montgomery County, Tennessee, from about 1835-6 until about 1846-7, when most of them moved to Weakley County. Records in both counties show their connections. For example, Ann Eliza Bradberry in Montgomery County named George W. And her brother Robert, who associated with John and David in Weakley County. John lived with or near James F. And his land adjoined Richard's farm. Henry's mother was "Ann," and Ann Eliza's mother was "Nancy," a nickname for Ann. Moreover, combining both counties' records provides enough information to identify these increasingly probable siblings in Virginia.

The Bradberry cluster in Virginia

Seven Bradberrys headed Virginia households in 1830. The names of two in King William County – Henry L. Bradberry and Ann Bradberry – echo those in Tennessee. The makeup of Henry's household matches the 1850 H. Bradberry household in Weakley County.

---

[22] Wade to Bradberry and Bradberry, Montgomery Co. Deed Book T: 151.

[23] Ann Eliza Bradberry will, Montgomery Co. Probate Record J: 321; FHL microfilm 0,321,048.

[24] Bradberry to Merriwether, Montgomery Co. Deed Book W: 274.

[25] Bradberry to Smith, Montgomery Co. Deed Book Y: 508; FHL microfilm 0,320,866.

[26] Bradberry entries, Montgomery Co. 1836 Tax List, District 1, p. 352, lines 15 (Richard) and 16 (Wm), and p. 353, lines 1 (John), 2 (John), 3 (Joseph), and 4 (Henry), Trustee, Clarksville, Tenn.; Early Tennessee Tax Lists microfilm 7, Tennessee State Library and Archives, Nashville.

[27] Montgomery County Court Minutes 21, District 2, entries 5 (Ric'd), 10 (Robert), and 11 (Wm), County Court, Clarksville, Tenn.; FHL microfilm 0,321,067. For a transcription see, County Court Minutes Book 21: An Enumeration of free white male persons in the county of Montgomery [in] 1841," *TNGenWeb Project* (http://www.tngenweb.org/montgomery/1841voters.html).

Although the 1830 census does not name most other Bradberry men in the Tennessee counties of Weakley and Montgomery, Ann Bradberry's household accounts for them. They include John Bradberry who, without information concerning his associates in Tennessee, could not have been identified in Virginia in 1830. See table 4.

Few records survived an 1885 courthouse fire in King William County.[28] Some refer to Bradberry court actions and deeds concerning John Bradberry who was about a generation older than the John of Tennessee:

- o John Bradberry, separately and jointly with Richard Bradberry, defended suits for debt in 1808, 1809, and 1820.[29]
- o On 24 June 1816 Richard Bradberry received payment for "patrolling" or other public activities.[30]
- o On 27 January 1817 Mary Garnett, a childless sister of John Bradberry's wife, named four of his daughters, Susanna, Polly, Lucy, and Jane Bradberry – names not appearing among the Tennessee Bradberrys.[31]
- o Earlier deeds identify John's wife as Frances Garnett, daughter of "Achiles" Garnett, and suggest that John married Frances soon after 1797.[32]
- o John Bradberry bought land in King William County in 1805 and 1810 and sold land there in 1811, 1816, and 1822.[33]

Like those of most "burned" Virginia counties, state copies of King William County's personal property and land tax records have survived.[34] They reveal details about the Bradberry cluster and their probable kin:

---

[28] John H. Gwathmey, *Twelve Virginia Counties: Where the Western Migration Began* (Baltimore Genealogical Publishing, 1979), 61.

[29] King William Co. Court Minute Book, pp. 81 (Richeson v. Richard and John Bradberry), 82 (Richeson v. John Bradberry), 183 (Richeson v. Richard and John Bradberry, continued), 253 (Hill v. John Bradberry and McNab), and 305 (Daniel v. Crow and Bradberry), Clerk of the County Court, King William, Va.; FHL microfilm 1,987,199, item 2.

[30] Ibid., unnumbered page near end of book.

[31] Garnett to Bradberry, King William Co. Deed Book 7:50, Clerk of the County Court, King William, Va.; FHL microfilm 1,987,190.

[32] Garnett to Fleet, King William Co. Deed Book 3:289; FHL microfilm 1,987,187. Bradberry to Smith, King William Co. Deed Book 6:22-23; FHL microfilm 1,988,189. Bradberry to Tuck, King William Co. Deed Book 8:398-99; FHL microfilm 1,987,191.

[33] King William Co. Deed Book 5:42 (Redd to McNab); FHL microfilm 1,987,188. King William Co. Deed Book 6:22-23 (Bradberry to Smith) and 104-6 (Garnett and others to Bradberry). King William Co. Deed Book 8:398-99 (Bradberry to Tirck); FHL microfilm 1,987,191. King William Co. Deed Book 8:466-6? (Temple to Bradberry) and 8:468-69 (Tompkins to Bradberry); FHL microfilm 1,987,192.

[34] See "Using Land Tax Records in the Archives at the Library of Virginia" and "Using Personal Property Taxes in the Archives of the Library of Virginia," Library of Virginia (http://www.lva.lib.va.us/whatwehave/land/m1-landtax.pdf) and (http://www.lva.lib.va.us/whatwehave/tax/m3_persprop.htm).

Table 3

**Suggested Composition of Bradberry Households in
Montgomery County, Tennessee, in 1840**

SEX AND AGE IN 1840	H.L. BRADBERRY	HOUSEHOLD RICHd BRADBERRY	MRS. A. BRADBERRY
MALES			
under 5	Edmond (2) Unknown	Unknown Unknown	
5-9	John (6) James (11)	Unknown	
20-29		Richard (28) Joseph (26)	Robert (24)
30-39	Henry (39)		
FEMALES			
under 5	Ann (5) Unknown	Ann (3) Unknown	
10-14	Georgeann (8)	Unknown Unknown	
15-19	Susan (12)		
15-19	Elizabeth (14)	Unknown	
20-29		Elizabeth (20)	Unknown
30-39	Susan (37)		
50-59			Mrs. A.

Sources: Richd Bradberry household, 1840 (J.S. census, Montgomery Co., Tenn., p. 264, line 23; H. L. Bradberry household, 1840 U.S. census, Montgomery Co., Tenn., p.267, line 29; and Mrs. A. Bradberry household, 1840 U.S. census, Montgomery Co., Tenn., p.268, line 11; all on National Archives (NA) microfilm M407, roll 532.
Note: Numerals in parentheses are ages in 1840 calculated from possibly corresponding entries in the 1850 census, whlch had the same enumeration date (1 June) as the 1840 census. See R. Bradberry, R. Bradberry, J. Bradberry and H. Bradberry households, 1850 U.S. census, Weakley Co., Tenn., pop. sch., Dist. 7, p. 468 (stamped, recto and verso), dwell./fam. 33, 36, 37, and 42, respectively; NA microfilm M432, roll 899. For the enumeration dates, see Ann Bruner Eales and Robert M. Kvasnicka, eds., "Census Records," in Genealogical Research in the National Archives of the United States, 3rd ed. (Washington, D.C.: National Archives and Records Administration, 2000), 24-25.

o John Bradberry paid taxes in King William County in 1800 through 1826, when tax liability for his land was transferred to Richard Bradberry "by deed."[35] Whether John died or moved away is unknown.

o Richard Bradberry was taxed in King William County in 1800-26. He died in 1826-27, as his estate was taxed in 1827-43.[36]

o Ann Bradberry was taxable in 1828-32.[37] She probably was Richard's widow because (1) she was taxed after his death, (2) his wife reportedly was "Ann," and (3) Ann Eliza Bradberry's mother was "Nancy" (a nickname for Ann).[38]

o Thomas Bradberry was taxable in 1817-19, suggesting that he had moved out on his own in 1817. The decrease from two polls to one in Richard Bradberry's 1816-17 listings suggests that Thomas was Richard's son. Richard's increase from one to two polls in 1813-14 implies the son turned sixteen in 1814.[39]

o Henry L. Bradberry paid taxes in 1820 and 1826-28.[40] The first listing indicates he was born before 1804, which is consistent with the Weakley County, Tennessee, "H. Bradberry" enumeration in 1850.[41]

o Robert Bradberry paid taxes in 1827, pointing to his birth before 1811, and agreeing with his Weakley County listing in 1850.[42]

o Except for the land in Richard's estate, tax listings for the above "free white" Bradberrys cease in 1834, consistent with the appearance of Bradberry families in Montgomery County, Tennessee.[43]

John and Richard Bradberry, both born 1776-94, headed King William County households in 1820. As shown in table 5, Richard's household configuration could include the Bradberrys who went to Tennessee. Considering only the composition of both households, however, either Richard or John could be their father. Two points tip the scale toward Richard:

---

[35]   John Bradberry entries, King William Co. 1800-1, 1804-7, and 1809-26 personal property tax lists and 1805-7 and 1809-26 land tax lists, unpaginated but alphabetized by first letter of surname, Virginia Commissioner of Revenue, Richmond; FHL microfilms 0,032,110 (personal property), 0,029,944 (land, 1805-19) and0,029,945 (land, 1870-26).

[36]   Richard Bradberry entries, King William Co. 1801, 1803, 1806, 1809, and 1811-26 personal property tax lists and 1826 land tax list. Richard Bradberry estate entries, King William Co. 1827-43 land tax lists.

[37]   Ann Bradberry entries, King William Co. 1828-32 personal property tax lists.

[38]   For Ann's identity as Richard Bradberry's wife, see Henry Bradberry family Bible record. For Nancy's identity as Ann Eliza Bradberry's mother, see Ann Eliza Bradberry will, Montgomery Co. Probate Record J:321.

[39]   King William Co. 1814 (Richard Bradberry), 1817 (Richard Bradberry and Thomas Bradberry), and 1818-19 (Thomas Bradberry) personal property tax lists.

[40]   Henry L. Bradberry entries, King William Co. 1820 and 1826-28 personal property tax lists.

[41]   H. Bradberry household, 1850 U.S. census, Weakley Co., Tenn., pop. sch., District 7, p. 468 (stamped, verso), dwell./fam. 42.

[42]   Robert Bradberry entry, King William Co. 1827 personal property tax list. R. Bradberry household 1850 U.S. census, Weakley Co., Tenn., pop. sch., District 7, p. 468 (stamped, recto), dwell./fam.36.

[43]   Several "free black" Bradbys and Bradberrys sporadically paid King William Co. personal property taxes between 1798 and 1841. Their given names were Edward, Miles, Ned, Patrick, Richard, and William.

o King William County tax and census evidence suggests John and his children left before 1830 and probably in 1826. In contrast, the Bradberrys appearing in Tennessee in 1838 remained in King William County through 1834.

o The King William County tax records imply that Ann was Richard's widow. Ann (or "Nancy") is identified directly as mother of two members of the cluster. Her household accounts for them in King William County in 1830.

Conclusion

King William County tax lists, its surviving courthouse records, and gleanings from the Tennessee counties of Montgomery and Weakley provide enough data to locate the Virginia origins and parents of John Bradberry who settled in Tennessee and Arkansas. Examining the pieces of evidence separately does not reveal John's parents or an origin more specific than "Virginia." Only when fragments of information about a cluster are assembled piece by piece does a picture emerge. Remarkably consistently, the bits support the hypothesis that the men in the Virginia-born cluster in 1850 Tennessee, including John, were born to Richard and Ann Bradberry in King William County, Virginia.

Perhaps the most common genealogical mistake is focusing a search too narrowly. Studying only John Bradberry and records he created would never have revealed his origin. Broadening research to include a cluster of migrating families, however led to convincing evidence of his birthplace and parents.

Table 4

Suggested Composition of Two Bradberry Households in King William County, Virginia, in 1830

	HOUSEHOLD	
SEX AND AGE IN 1830	ANN BRADBERRY	HENRY BRADBERRY
Males		
under 5		James (a)
5-9	David (of age in 1848) (b)	
10-14	Robert (14)	
15-19	Joseph (16) Richard S. (18)	
20-30	James F. (20-30) (c) William W. (of age in 1836) (d) John (20)	Henry (30)
Females		
under 5		Elizabeth (4) Susan (2)
5-9		Virginia (6)
10-14	Ann Eliza (e)	
15-19		Elizabeth (14)
20-29	unknown	
50-59	Ann	

Source: Ann Bradberry household, 1830 U.S. census, King William Co., Va., p. 92, line 23; Henry L Bradberry household, 1830 U.S. census, King William Co., Va., p. 86, line 26; both on National Archives (NA) microfilm M19, roll 201.

(a) Numerals in parentheses are ages in 1830 calculated from entries in the 1850 census, which had the same enumeration date (1 June) as the 1830 census. See See R. Bradberry, R. Bradberry, J. Bradberry, and H. Bradberry households, 1850 U.S. census, Weakley Co., Tenn., pop. sch., Dist. 7, p. 468 (stamped, recto and verso), dwell./fam. 33, 36,.37, and 42, respectively; NA microfilm M432, ro11.899.

(b) David Bradberry entry, 1848, district 7, Weakley Co. Tax Book 2, County Tiustee, Dresden, Tenn.; microfilm 1,003,115, Family History Library, Salt Lake City.

(c) Jas F Bradberry household, 1840 U.S. census, l7eakley Co., Tenn., p. 297, line 27; NA microfilm M704, roll 530; shows James as age 30-39.

(d) Wm Bradberry entry, Montgomery Co. 1836 tax list, District l, p.352, line 16; Early Tennessee Tax Lists microfilm 7, Tennessee State Library and Archives, Nashville.

(e) If Ann Eliza was the unknown female age20-29 in the Mrs. A. Bradberry household in 1840, which seems likely, she was age 10-19 in 1830. See Mrs. A. Bradberry household, 1840 U.S. census, Montgomery Co., Tenn., p. 268, line 11; NA microfilm M407, roll 532.

Table 5

Suggested composition of Richard Bradberry Household in 1820

SEX AND AGE	IDENTITIES
Males	
under 10	Robert (4) (a)
	Joseph (6)
	Richard S. (8)
	John (10)
10-14	William W. (of age in 1836) (b)
	James F. (10-20) (c)
	Henry (20)
26-44	Richard
Females	
under 10	Ann Eliza (d)
16-26	Unknown
26-44	Ann ("Nancy")

Source: Richard Bradbury household, 1820 U.S. census, King William Co., Va., p.334, line 8; National Archives (NA) microfilm M33, roll 136.

a. Numerals in parentheses are ages in 1820 calculated from entries in the 1850 census, which had the same enumeration date (1 June) as the 1820 census. See R. Bradberry R. Bradberry J. Bradberry, and H. Bradberry households, 1850 U.S. census, Weakley Co., Tenn., pop. sch., District 7, p. 468 (stamped, recto and verso), dwells/fams 33, 36, 37, and 42, respectively; NA microfilm M43), roll 899. For enumeration dates see Ann Bruner Eales and Robert M. Kvasnicka, eds., "Census Records," in Gercalogical Research in the Nationnl Archives of the United Sr,ares, 3rd ed. (Washington, D.C.: National Archives and Records Administration, 2000), 24-25.

b. Wm Bradberry entry Montgomery Co. 1836 tax list, District 1, p. 352, line 16; Early Tennessee Tax Lists microfilm 7, Tennessee State Library and Archives, Nashville.

c. Jas F Bradberry household, 1840 U.S. census, Weakley Co., Tenn., p. 292, M704, roll 530; shows James as age 30-39.

d. If Ann Eliza was the unknown female age 2O-29 in the Mrs. A. Bradberry household in 1840, which seems likely, she was under age 10 in 1820. See Mrs. A. Bradberry househoid, i840 U.S. census, Montgomery Co., Tenn., p.768, line 11; NA microfilm M407, roll 532.

Genealogical Summary

1. **Richard Bradberry** was born about 1775.[44] He died in King William County, Virginia, in 1826-77.[45] Richard married Ann "Nancy" (née [-?-]), probably before 1797 if she was mother of all his children.[46] Born about 1780, Ann headed a household in King William County in 1830 and Montgomery County, Tennessee, in 1840.[47] She died after 22 November 1843, probably in Tennessee.[48] The evidence discussed above suggests that Richard had eleven children, born in King William County:

2   i. Thomas Bradberry, born about 1797-98.[49] By 1830 he had settled in Augusta County, Virginia, with a young household.[50]

3   ii. Henry L. Bradberry, born 1 April 1801. On 15 April 18?l, probably in King William County, he married Susan Thylor, born 7 April 1803 to James and Genie Taylor.[51]

4   iii. William T. Bradberry, born about 1805-10.[52] He married on 19 November 1839 in Montgomery County, Ann Ragsdale.[53]

---

[44]   Richard Bradbury household, 1820 U.S. census, King William Co., Va., p. 314, line 8; NA microfilm M33, roll 136.

[45]   King William Co. 1826 (Richard Bradberry) and 1827 (Richard Bradberry estate) land tax lists.

[46]   For Ann's identity as Richard Bradberry's wife, see Henry Bradberry family Bible record. For her nickname "Nancy," see Ann Eliza Bradberry will, Montgomery Co. Probate Record J: 321.

[47]   Ann Bradberry household, 1830 U.S. census, King William Co., Va., p. 92, line 23. Mrs. A. Bradberry household, 1840 U.S. census, Montgomery Co., Tenn., p. 268, line 11; NA microfilm M407, roll 532.

[48]   Ann Eliza Bradberry will, Montgomery Co. Probate Record J: 321.

[49]   King William Co. 1814 (Richard Bradberry) and 1817 (Richard Bradberry and Thomas Bradberry) personal property tax lists.

[50]   Thomas Bradberry household, 1830 U.S. census, Augusta Co., Va., p. 70, line 3; NA microfilm M19, roll 189.

[51]   Henry Bradberry family Bible record. The record includes birth dates for Henry's older children: Virginia A., 22 November 1824; Elizabeth, 25 July 1826; Susan, 7 February 1828; James, 2 March 1830; and George Enor, 25 December 1831.

[52]   Richard Bradbury household, 1820 U.S. census, King William Co., Va., p. 314, line 8. Ann Bradberry household, 1830 U.S. census, King William Co., Va., p. 97, line 23. William is not named in either census; his enumeration is inferred from his associations with the Bradberry cluster.

[53]   Bradberry-Ragsdale marriage record, Montgomery Co. Marriage Record 1:25, County Court, Clarksville, Tenn.; FHL microfilm 0,321,021.

5   iv. James F. Bradberry, born about 1805-10.[54]

6   v. John N. Bradberry, born 1809-10. He married, apparently, Sarah A. (née [-?-]), who was born in North Carolina, 1820-21.[55]

7   vi. Richard S. Bradberry, born 1811-12. He married, apparently, Elizabeth (née [-?-]), born in Tennessee in 1809-10.[56]

8   vii. Joseph C. Bradberry, born 1813-14.[57] On 10 September 1852 in Weakley County, Tennessee, he married Mary Ford.[58]

9   viii. Robert Semple Bradberry, born 28 September 1816; died 20 March 1875.[59] On 24 December 1846 in Montgomery County he married Elizabeth Ann Ford.[60] Daughter of James and Nancy Ford, she was born in Montgomery County on 22 October 1828.[61]

10   ix. Ann Eliza Bradberry, born 1816-20.[62] She died unmarried in Montgomery County, between 22 November 1843 and February 1846.[63]

11   x. George W. Bradberry, born 25 December 1822; died 8 February 1881.[64] On 18 January 1846 in Montgomery County, he married Sarah E. O'Neal.[65] Sarah was born 19 December 1828 and died 20 August

---

[54]   Richard Bradbury household, 1820 U.S. census, King William Co., Va., p. 314, line 8. Ann Bradberry household, 1830 U.S. census, King William Co., Va., p. 92, line 23. James is not named in either census; his enumeration is inferred from his associations with the Bradberry cluster.

[55]   J. Bradberry household, 1850 U.S. census, Weakley Co., Tenn., pop. sch., District 7, p. 468 (stamped, recto), dwell.fam. 37. John Bradberry household, 1860 U.S. census, Greene Co., Ark., pop. sch., Concord Twp., Oak Bluff post office, p.112, dwell. 670, fam. 655.J. N. Bradbery household, 1870 U. S. census, Greene Co., Ark., pop. sch., Johnson Twp., Big Creek post office, p. 8, dwell./fam. 52.

[56]   R. Bradberry household 1850 U.S. census, (stamped, recto), dwell./fam. 36. District 7, p. 468.

[57]   J. C. Bradbery household, 1870 U.S. census, Weakley Co., Tenn., pop. sch., Civil District 2, Dresden post office, p. 12, dwell./fam. 72; NA microfilm M593, roll 1570. Joseph Bradbury household, 1880 U.S. census, Clay Co., Ark., pop. sch., Bradshaw Twp., ED 32, sheet 23, dwell. 188, fam. 193; NA microfilm T9, roll 40.

[58]   Bradberry-Ford marriage record, Weakley Co. Marriage Records 1843-66,p. 28, County Court Clerk, Dresden, Tenn.; FHL microfilm 0,988,668.

[59]   "Bradberry Cemetery," in Daughters of the American Revolution James Buckley Chapter, Weakley county, Tennessee: cemetery listings, 2 vols. (Sharon, Tenn., 1980), 1:39.

[60]   Bradberry-Ford marriage record, Montgomery co. Marriage Record 1: 25.

[61]   Robert Semple Bradbury family Bible record , in Old and New Testament translated, out of original tongues in Philadelphia (Philadelphia: John E. Potter, no publication date); photocopy by Carolyn Wilcoxen in author's files.

[62]   If Ann Eliza was the unknown female in the Mrs. A. Bradberry household in 1840, which seems likely, she was born 1810-20. Correlating that entry with those of females of comparable age in likely Bradberry households in 1830 and 1820 yields 1816-20 as the probable time of her birth. See Mrs. A. Bradbury household, 1840 U.S. census, Montgomery Co., Tenn., p.268, line 11. Also, Richard Bradbury household, 1820 U.S. census, King William Co., Va., p. 314, line 8; and Ann Bradberry household, 1830 U.S. census, King William Co., Va., p. 92, line 23.

[63]   Ann Eliza Bradberry will, Montgomery co. probate Record J: 321.

[64]   Anita Whitefield Darnell et al., Cemetery Records of Montgomery County, Tennessee,3 vols. (Clarksville, Tenn.: Ideal Publishing, 1965-68), 1: 61.

[65]   Bradberry-O'Neal marriage record, Montgomery Co. Marriage Record 1: 14.

1879.[66] George remained in Montgomery County after most of his brothers moved to Weakley County.[67]

12   xi. David Bradberry, born 1826-27.[68]

---

[66]   Darnell et. al., *Cemetery Records of Montgomery county, Tennessee*, l: 61.

[67]   Geo. W. Bradbery household, 1850 U.S. census, Montgomery Co., Tenn., pop. sch. [district not specified], p.223 (stamped, verso), dwell./fam. 1312; NA microfilm M432, roll 891. G. W. Bradbury household, 1860 U.S. census, Montgomery Co., Tenn., pop. sch., "N & E of Cumberland River," Clarksville post office, p. 390, dwell./fam. 482; NA microfilm M593, roll 1266.

[68]   David Bradberry entry, list for 1848, Civil District 7, Weakley Co. Tax Book 2, unpaginated but alphabetical within each district, County Trustee, Dresden, Tenn.; FHL microfilm 1,003,115.

Chapter 10

Explaining the Sudden Disappearance of
Mitch Evins of Georgia and Texas[1]

Mitch's disappearance and his life afterward remained a mystery.

Public records rarely specify people's reasoning. Reconstructing a life from birth to death, however, may reveal enough for a family historian to ascribe motives. Family pressures and problems, for example, likely caused Mitch Evins to do the seemingly inexplicable:

Mitch Evins is said to have been one-quarter Cherokee Indian, and had many Indian ways. He would much rather hunt and fish than work at anything else, and he did hate to wear a hat. His wife tried to civilize him, and he did very well. He even went to Church, driving his wife and children quite regularly. The story goes that one Sunday morning he had curried the horses well, put them to the surrey and drove around to the front gate where he hitched them to go into the house and get ready. He came through the gate, turned to shut it, and stopped to look over the countryside. Suddenly, he jerked his hat off, threw it into the path and jumped on it! He then re-opened the gate and walked out. His family never saw him again.[2]

Mitch's disappearance and his life afterward remained a mystery. Where did he go and why? Did he commit a crime? Was he disgraced? Was his alleged Cherokee heritage correct? If so, did it create conflict with his neighbors?

---

[1] "Explaining the Sudden Disappearance of Mitch Evins of Texas and Georgia," *The National Genealogical Society Quarterly*, Vol 102, #1, March 2014, pp 41-50.

[2] Iola Harriet Bird Embry, undated typescript, privately held; digital transcription in author's files. Mrs. Embry (1895-1967), wife of Thomas Mitchell Evins's great-grandson, was a family historian.

Early years

Thomas Mitchell "Mitch" Evins (or Evans) was born on 17 January 1820 in Franklin County, Georgia, to John Leroy Evins and Nancy Baugh.[3] They had married there on 28 March 1817.[4]

When Mitch was an infant the Evinses left Franklin County.[5] Mitch's father next appears in DeKalb County, Georgia, in 1828, when he and four other men purchased land for a Methodist church.[6] The family likely had relocated around 1822, when DeKalb County was formed.[7] They settled on the banks of a creek later called Nancy Creek, perhaps after Mitch's mother.[8]

Violence and murder

Some of Mitch's relatives were unusually violent. In 1842 Mitch's eldest brother George Washington "Wash" Evins struck Allen Haraman and shoved him to the ground. During the ensuing excitement Mitch's father kicked Allen, breaking two ribs. Arrested and charged with assault and battery, father and son pleaded guilty. The court fined them each twenty-five dollars plus costs.[9] Seven times over the next few years in DeKalb superior court

[3] Franklin Garrett, transcription of "family bible of Justinian Evins in the possession of his daughter, Mrs. F. B. Maddox," two pages, 11 May 1950; Franklin Garrett manuscripts, Kenan Research Center; Atlanta History Center (AHC), Atlanta, Ga.; AHC Franklin Garrett Necrology microfilm 5, frames 252–53.

[4] Franklin Co., Ga., Record of Marriage Licenses, transcription, 1851, p. 134, Ivins-Baugh, issued 28 January 1817; Court of Ordinary, Carnesville, Ga.; microfilm 7,119, Family History Library (FHL), Salt Lake City. Original licenses for 1817 survive, but the Ivins-Baugh license seems unfindable. See Franklin Co., Ga., marriage records 1806–1905, alphabetical by groom's surname, folders 46, Easley–Ellison; 47, Elrod–Evett; and 75, Ingram–Ivery; Georgia Department of Archives and History (GDAH), Morrow; FHL microfilm 2,188,706. The cited folders contain marriage documents for Franklin County grooms with surnames beginning with *E* and *I*.

[5] Franklin Co., tax digest, 1820, pp. 43, Captain Brus district, John Ivins (land in Franklin and Wayne Co.) and 47, Captain A. Yancey's district John Ivins Jur (poll only); GDAH; FHL microfilm 159,145. Ibid., 1821, unpaginated, Captain Duncan's district, John Evans (land in Franklin and Wayne Co.), and Captain Yancey's district, John Evans (land in Appling Co.) For John Evans/Evans/Ivins's absence as a Franklin County taxpayer after 1821, see Martha Walters Acker, *Franklin County, Georgia, Tax Digests*, 4 vols. (Birmingham, Ala.: privately printed, 1980–87), 3:270 (covering 1819–23) and 4:315 (for 1825–39).

[6] DeKalb Co., Ga., Deed Book H:206–7, Eaton to Mangum and others, 1 February 1828; Superior Court, Decatur, Ga.; FHL microfilm 365,313.

[7] DeKalb County tax digests, which might pinpoint the family's settlement there, do not predate 1848. See "Collection Overview: Revenue – Property Tax Unit – County Property Tax digests, 1793–2000," *Finding Aids @ Georgia Archives: Online Descriptive Inventories for Government Records Series* (http://find.georgiaarchives.org/archon/index.php?p=collections /findingaid&id=3984&rootcontentid=114345&q=dekalb#id114345). For DeKalb County's formation, see William C. Dawson, comp., *Compilation of the Laws of the State of Georgia Passed by the General Assembly, since the Year 1819 to the Year 1829, Inclusive* (Milledgeville, Ga.: Grantland and Orme, 1831), 122–23, "An Act to Organize the Counties of De Kalb, Pike, Crawford, and Bibb."

[8] Franklin M. Garrett, in *Atlanta and Environs: A Chronicle of Its People and Events*, 3 vols. (New York: Lewis, 1954), 1:42, writes "The homeplace was in land lot 13, very close to the present intersection of Peachtree-Dunwoody and House roads and overlooking the valley of Nancy Creek." Also, Vivian Price, *The History of DeKalb County, Georgia, 1822–1900* (Fernandina Beach, Fla.: Wolf, 1997), 109.

[9] DeKalb Co., Minutes A:356–57, September term 1842, and A:402 and 422, March term 1843; FHL microfilm 365,297.

they addressed charges of assault, assault and battery, and assault with intent to murder.[10] Mitch's brother Milton F. Evins appeared once for assault with intent to murder.[11] On 24 November 1852 Mitch's father, John, and some of his sons attended an estate sale in DeKalb County.[12] There, Mitch's brother Wash argued with James Lowery Jr., pulled a gun, and killed him.[13] Arrested and charged with murder, Wash pleaded not guilty.[14]

Within a year, on 28 September 1853, Wash escaped from jail. Twelve days later Georgia's governor issued a proclamation offering one-hundred-fifty dollars for recapturing him.[15] Mitch's younger brother, Crawford, pleaded not guilty to charges of assault and battery and assisting Wash to escape.[16] Almost five years later, in April 1857, he was cleared of the charge of assisting the escape.[17] Wash evaded capture for at least twenty-three years.[18]

Adulthood and indebtedness

Compared with his father and brothers, Mitch was peaceful. On 5 February 1839 he married Mary Emeline Collier, likely in DeKalb County.[19] Between December 1841 and May 1845 they had three children—Caroline, Justinian, and Emeline.[20] In 1839 and 1842 Mitch witnessed deeds for his father.[21] In 1844 he served on a DeKalb county Superior court grand jury.[22]

---

[10]   Ibid., B:44, September term 1844 (2 incidents); B:107 and 133, March term 1845; B:114, September term 1845; B:121 and 133, September term 1845; B:252, March term 1846; B:151–2, March term 1846; B:174 and 176–77, September term 1846; B:196, March term 1847; and B:326, September term 1849. Also, ibid., C:106, October Term 1852; FHL microfilm 265,298.

[11]   Ibid., B:514, September term, 1851.

[12]   DeKalb Co., Inventories, Annual Returns, Bills of Sales, Vouchers, Appraisements B:114; Court of Ordinary, Decatur; FHL microfilm 365,281.

[13]   Joe Reeves, interview by Franklin Garrett, 1931; Franklin Garrett manuscripts, Atlanta History Center; Franklin Garrett necrology microfilm 1, frame 107. For Lowery, see 1850 U.S. census, DeKalb Co., Ga., population schedule, Cross Keys District, p. 227, folio 114r, dwelling/family 85, James Lowery household; National Archives and Records Administration (NARA) microfilm M432, roll 67.

[14]   DeKalb Co., Superior Court Minutes C:106, October term (arrest), C:123, April 1853 term (arraignment and plea), and C; FHL microfilm 365,298.

[15]   "A Proclamation, Georgia, by Howell Cobb, Governor of said State," *Federal Union*, Milledgeville, Ga., page 3, col. 5. Also, *The Southern Recorder*, Milledgeville, Ga., page 3, col. 6.

[16]   DeKalb Co., Superior Court Minutes, C:167, April 1853 term (assault and battery); C:273, October 1853 term (escape);and C:297 and 396, October 1853 term (pleas). The charge of assisting a prisoner to escape is headed with the name of George W. Evins, though Crawford Evins was accused.

[17]   Ibid., C:543, April 1857 term.

[18]   "Town Topics," *Atlanta Constitution*, 15 April 1876, page 3, col. 3.

[19]   Without documentation, lineage society applications give this marriage date. See, for example, *Ancestry* (http://www.ancestry.com) > U.S., Sons of the American Revolution Membership Applications, 1889-1970 > image 135, membership application of Thornton Melville Fincher (national no. 78829), approved 16 December 1954, National Society Sons of the American Revolution. Also, membership application of Cynthia Diane Crawford Kentucky (national no. 914664), accepted 2 February 2013; National Society Daughters of the American Revolution, Office of the Registrar General, Washington, D.C. A courthouse fire on 8 January 1842 destroyed DeKalb County's prior marriage records. See Paul K. Graham, *Georgia Courthouse Disasters* (Decatur, Ga: Genealogy Co., 2013), 26–27,

[20]   Garrett, transcription of "family bible of Justinian Evins."

[21]   Gordon Co., Ga., Deeds and Mortgages B:381–82, Smith to Evins, 8 January 1839; Superior Court, Calhoun, Ga.; FHL microfilm 422,608. Also, DeKalb Co., Ga., Deeds H:124–25, McBee to Evins, 26 November 1842; Superior Court, Decatur, Ga.; FHL microfilm 365,313.

[22]   DeKalb Co., Minutes B:34, 36, and 74, September term, 1844; Superior Court; FHL microfilm 365,297.

By 1848, when Mitch's fourth child, Georgia, was born, his family had settled near Calhoun, Gordon County, Georgia. They soon had another son, John, and a daughter, Jamie.[23] In 1850 they lived in or near Calhoun.[24] They owned a seventeen-year-old black female and a one-year-old mulatto girl.[25] Possibly Mitch fathered the child. Mitch paid taxes in Gordon County in 1851–53 on land in several Georgia counties.[26]

While living in Gordon County, Mitch bought, mortgaged, and sold land:

o On 29 August 1850 he paid one hundred dollars for land in Union County, Georgia.[27] On 10 November he sold it for the same amount.[28]

o He purchased forty acres in Floyd County, Georgia, on 21 August 1852.[29] He sold it on 27 April 1853.[30]

o On 5 November 1853 he mortgaged four lots in Gordon County for two hundred dollars. He paid off the note on 15 March 1854.[31]

Mitch's repeated indebtedness led to court actions:

o In May 1851 he and two others were held liable for a six-hundred-dollar bond for Mitch's failure to appear at court.[32] In March 1852 the court ruled against the three men for costs.[33]

o On 12 April 1854 a Gordon County judge authorized the sheriff to collect thirty dollars plus court and collection costs from Mitch, in debt to a Calhoun business. Mitch had left the county, however, and the sheriff collected nothing. The court concluded the case on 12 November 1858, when the sheriff foreclosed on Mitch's land in Gordon County, selling it for fifty dollars.[34]

o In September 1855 Mitch and four others lost $327 principal plus interest and

---

[23]   Garrett, transcription of "family bible of Justinian Evins."

[24]   . 1850 U.S. census, Gordon Co., Ga., pop. sch., Divison 12, p. 33, dwell. 95, fam. 96 Thomas M. Evans household; NARA microfilm M432, roll 71.

[25]   1850 U.S. census, Gordon Co., Ga., slave sched., Division 12, p. 2, Thos M Erv$_{in}$; NARA microfilm M432, roll 90. *Ervin* likely is an error for *Evans*. Joseph Wilson was enumerated next to Thomas W. Evans in the population schedule and Thos M Ervin in the slave schedule.

[26]   Gordon Co., Tax Digest, 1851, unpaginated, district 7, T. M. Evins (land in counties of Baker, Decatur, Taliaferro, and Thomas); Court of Ordinary, Calhoun; FHL microfilm 422,604. Also, ibid., 1852, unpaginated, district 7, Thos. M. Evins (land in Gordon Co.); and 1853, unpaginated, district 14, Tho$^{s. M. Ev}$ans (land in counties of Floyd, Gilmer, Polk, and Union); GDHA; FHL microfilm 159,150. items 2–3.

[27]   Union Co., Ga., Deeds J:669, Faggans to Evins; Superior Court, Blairsville, Ga.; FHL microfilm 366,314.

[28]   Ibid., Evins to Lewis.

[29]   Floyd Co., Ga., Deed Book AA:258–59, Wylie to Evins, 21 August 1852; Superior Court, Rome, Ga; FHL microfilm 282,533.

[30]   Ibid., AA:259–60, Evins to Ross, 28 April 1853. The buyer presented the deed in court on 21 February 1854, and witness Francis M. Allen swore that he saw Evins sign it. This deed, the prior one, and two later deeds for the same property were filed and recorded on 21 March 1881. See ibid, AA:260–61, Ross to Cooper, 14 September 1856, and AA:261–22, heirs at law of Cooper to Tecumseh Iron Co., 4 March 1881.

[31]   Gordon Co., Deeds and Mortgages B:280–81, Evins to Stroup.

[32]   Gordon Co., Superior court minutes A, unpaginated, May term 1851; Superior Court, Calhoun; FHL microfilm 424,321

[33]   Ibid., March term 1852.

[34]   Gordon Co., Deeds and Mortgages D:421–22, Hudgins to Reed, 5 December 1858; FHL microfilm 422,610.

costs.[35] They paid the costs and appealed. A month later they lost again.[36]

 o In October 1858 a court required to Mitch to pay costs and two hundred dollars he owed Thomas Blackburn.[37]

In 1853 Fulton County was created from the western half of DeKalb County.[38] In 1854 Mitch sold his Floyd County land, and the next year his Polk County land.[39] Mitch's last two children—Frances and Minerva—were born in Fulton County.[40] He paid taxes there in 1855.[41] Mitch soon "jerked his hat off ... and walked out."

Mitch's wife Emeline never saw him again. In July 1860 she—reportedly a "Widow"—and eight children still lived in Fulton County.[42] In 1870, using her maiden name, she still lived there.[43] In 1880 she ran an Atlanta boarding house.[44] As "Evins Emaline (wid T M)," she subsequently moved several times within the city.[45] In 1900 and 1910 she lived with her daughter Frances Henrietta Lee.[46] Emeline celebrated her ninety-second birthday on 1 October 1912.[47] Shortly thereafter she fell and broke her hip. She died on 21 February 1913.[48]

A second Gordon County Thomas Evins/Evans?

After Mitch settled in Fulton County, T. M. or Thos M. Evins paid tax in Gordon County. He paid taxes in 1858–61, in a different tax district from Mitch, and owned no

[35] Gordon Co., Superior Court Minutes B, unpaginated, 24 September 1855, Duglass v. Evins and others, debt; FHL microfilm 424,321.

[36] Ibid., B, 2 October 1855, appeal.

[37] Ibid., C, unpaginated, 14 October 1858, Blackburn v. Evans and Neal; FHL microfilm 424,322.

[38] *Acts of the General Assembly of the State of Georgia, Passed in Milledgeville at a Biennial Session in November, December, January, and February 1853–4* (Savannah: Samuel T. Chapman: 1854), 300.

[39] Floyd Co., Deeds J:425, Evins to Ayers; FHL microfilm 282,517. Also, Polk Co., Ga., Deed Book B:123, Evins to Willingham; Superior Court, Cedartown, Ga.; FHL microfilm 419,262.

[40] Garrett, transcription of "family bible of Justinian Evins.

[41] *Ancestry.com* (http://www.ancestry.com) > Georgia, Property Tax Digests, 1793–1892 > Fulton > 1855 > digital image 32, Fulton Co. Ga., Tax Digest, 1855, District 1026, arranged by first letter of taxpayer's surname, Thomas M. Evans (land in Union Co.).

[42] 1860 U.S. census, Fulton Co., Ga., pop. sch., Cooks Dist., p. 216, dwell 1428, fam. 1532, Emaline Evans household; NARA microfilm M653, roll 123.

[43] 1870 U.S. census, Fulton Co., Ga., pop. sch., Atlanta post office, p. 85, dwell. 718, fam. 691, Emaline Collier household; NARA microfilm M593, roll 151.

[44] 1880 U.S. census, Fulton Co., Ga., pop. sch., Atlanta, enumeration district (ED) 103, p. 33, dwell 175, fam. 232, Emeline Evans household; NARA microfilm T9, roll 148.

[45] *Sholes' Directory of the City of Atlanta for 1880* (Atlanta: A. E. Sholes, 1880), 184. Also, ibid., *1881*, p. 244. Also, *Atlanta Georgia City Directory 1883* (Atlanta: Weatherbe, 1883), 291. Also, *Weatherbe's Atlanta Georgia Duplex City Directory 1885* (Atlanta: Weatherbe, 1885), 187. Also, *Atlanta City Directory for 1888* (Atlanta: Constitution, 1888), 493. Also, ibid., *1889*, p. 512; *1893*, p. 577; *1896*, p. 661; *1898*, p. 630; *1899*, p. 699; *1900*, p. 699; and 1901, p. 720.

[46] 1900 U.S. census, Fulton Co., Ga., pop. sch., Atlanta, ED 65, sheet 30A, dwell 537, fam. 606, Charles J. Lee household; NARA microfilm T623, roll 199. Also, 1910 U.S. census, Fulton Co., Ga., pop. sch., Atlanta, Ward 4, ED 71, sheet 34B, dwell. 172, fam. 245, Charles J. Lee household; NARA microfilm T624, roll microfilm 191.

[47] "Birthday Celebration," *Atlanta Constitution*, 1 October 1912, page 8, col. 2.

[48] Obituary of Mrs. Emmiline Collier Evans, unidentified newspaper clipping, Atlanta, Ga., 22 February 1913; author's files. Also, *Atlanta Constitution*, 22 February 1913, page 2, col. 3. Also, "Death Notice," *Atlanta Constitution*, 23 February 1913, page A12, col. 6.

land.[49] In 1860 this South Carolina native, a wagon maker, was still landless. His wife, Martha, was born in North Carolina, and his five children in South Carolina.[50] Ten years earlier they lived in Pickens District, South Carolina.[51] In 1870 this Thomas Evans, now fifty-seven, lived alone in Lee, Illinois, still landless.[52] He was not Mitch.

Mitch reappears

Mitch appears in no known Georgia record after the 1850s. In 1860 forty-year-old "Thomas M. Evans" born in Franklin County, Georgia, was farming in Jackson County, Texas—a perfect match to Emeline Evins's missing husband, born in Franklin County in 1820.[53] The Texas man reportedly owned real estate worth one thousand dollars.[54] Jackson County land records do not show that Mitch owned land there.[55]

Mitch may have followed brother, John C. Evins, to Texas. John, a lawyer and official at Laredo, had gone to Texas after his law training in Georgia.[56] At Laredo in 1862 Mitch, enlisting in Duff's Partisan Rangers, provided a forty-dollar horse and twenty-five dollars of equipment, including a saddle.[57]

He quickly rose to responsible positions. On 30 April 1862 Mitch served as clerk in the quartermaster's department. On 10 August he was "elected from the ranks" to first lieutenant. At the end of September he purchased supplies for his unit from several local suppliers, including his brother. On 6 October he traveled three-hundred-sixty miles to and from San Antonio to procure "subsistence stores and commissary funds" for Laredo. He received reimbursement of ten cents per mile. On 30 November Mitch signed the 30 November muster roll as "commanding company."[58]

After his discharge Mitch settled in Brownsville, Texas. In 1867–69 he was a voter in the city's precinct five, reportedly a ten-year Texas resident in the county and precinct

---

[49]   Gordon Co., Tax Digests, district 6, alphabetical by first letter of taxpayer's surname, 1858, T. M. Evans; 1859, T. M. Evins; 1860, T N Evins; 1861, Tho[s] M EV[ins]; FHL microfilm 422,604.

[50]   1860 U.S. census, Gordon Co., Ga., pop. sch., Sonora, p. 24, dwell 521, fam. 503, Thomas M. Evans household; NARA microfilm M653, roll 124.

[51]   1850 U.S. census, Pickens Co., S.C., pop. sch., Western Division, p. 102, dwell 759, fam. 797, Thomas M. Evans household; NARA microfilm M432, roll 857.

[52]   1870 U.S. census, Brown Co., Ill., pop. sch., Lee Twp., p. 33, dwell./fam. 232, Thomas Evans household; NARA microfilm M593, roll 189.

[53]   1860 U.S. census, Jackson Co., Tex., pop. sch., Morales de la Vaca, p. 35, dwell./fam. 254, W. S. Crawson household; NARA microfilm M653, roll 1298. The enumerator recorded each person's county and state of birth.

[54]   Ibid.

[55]   Jackson Co, Tex., Index to Deeds, A–G, direct and reverse, 1836 and 1840–1918, read for Evans and Evins; County Court, Edna, Tex.; FHL microfilms 1,010,493 and 1,010, 496.

[56]   "Mr. John C. Evans," *Atlanta Constitution*, 20 July 1898, page 42, col. 7. Also, 1860 U.S. census, Webb Co., Tex., pop. sch., Laredo, p. 10/73, dwell. 660/73, fam. 673/74, John C. Evans household; NARA microfilm M653, roll 1308. Also, "Final Call comes to John C. Evins." *Atlanta Constitution*, 29 December 1909, page 2, col. 3.

[57]   *Compiled Service Records of Confederate Soldiers Who Served in Organizations from the State of Texas,* microfilm publication M323, 445 rolls (Washington, D.C., NARA, 1963), roll 162, for Thomas M. Evins (private and lieutenant, company H, 33 Texas Cavalry [Duff's Partisan Rangers, 14th Battalion Cavalry], Civil War), eight cards. His age in 1862 was forty-two.

[58]   Ibid.

since 1864–66.[59] He was a jailer in Brownsville in 1870.[60]

Mitch seemingly disappeared for the next twenty years.[61] Perhaps he lived in Mexico. In 1904 his son, John H. Evins, lived in Monterey, Mexico, about 180 miles west of Brownsville.[62] John died there in 1910.[63]

In 1891 Mitch arrived in Cleburne, Johnson County, Texas. In poor health, he lived at the county poor farm. In response to state legislation enacted on 12 May 1899, he applied for a Confederate veteran's pension. He said he was seventy-nine years old and seven months, that he had lived in Johnson County for eight years, and that he was "very feeble" and unable to work. His signature is still easily recognizable.[64] He died on 9 July 1900, just ten months after his application was approved. Somehow his family in Georgia received word of his death.[65] Mitch's remains were buried in the poor farm cemetery.[66]

Cherokee ancestry?

In 1896 twelve of Mitch's descendants applied to the Dawes Commission for Cherokee citizenship.[67] In 1907 and 1909 forty-three Evins descendants applied to the Guion Miller Commission.[68] Mitch's brother, John C. Evins, stated the family's case:

---

[59] Texas Secretary of State, Voter Registration Lists, 1867–1869, Texas State Archives Collection; Texas State Library and Archives (TSLA), Austin; TSLA microfilm VR-2, for Cameron Co., p. 21, line 19.

[60] 1870 U.S. census, Cameron Co., Tex., pop. sch., Brownsville, Ward 1, p. 46, dwell. 504, fam. 479, Thomas Evans; NARA microfilm M593, roll 1578.

[61] Mitch has not been found in Texas in 1880 and 1900. See "1880 United States Federal Census" and "1900 United States Federal Census,"*Ancestry.com*, searches for surname *Ev?ns*, living in Texas but born in Georgia in 1810–30. Also, "Records" *FamilySearch* (familysearch.org/search), search *Thomas Evans* and *Mitch Evans*, born in Georgia in 1810–30.

[62] "Social Items," *Atlanta Constitution*, 16 September 1904, page 8, col. 2.

[63] Garrett, transcription of "family bible of Justinian Evins.

[64] *Ancestry.com* > U.S., Confederate Pensions, 1884–1958 > Texas > Pension Files Nos. 01537 to 03030 > Pension File Nos. 02311 to 02395 Application Years 1889 to 1929 > images 58–66, Thomas M. Evins file.

[65] Garrett, transcription of "family bible of Justinian Evins."

[66] Johnson County History Book Committee, *The History of Johnson County, Texas* (Dallas: Curtis, 1985), 17–19. In 1963 construction of Pat Cleburne Reservoir threatened the cemetery, and all its interred remains were reburied in the Cleburne city cemetery, Rose Hill. See Laretta Laurents (Library Assistant, Cleburne Public Library), e-mail to author, 13 February 2007; author's files

[67] *Applications from the Bureau of Indian Affairs, Muskogee Area Office, Relating to Enrollment in the Five Civilized Tribes under the Act of 1896*, microfilm publication M1650, 54 rolls (Washington, D.C.: NARA, 1992), roll 37, application 2801 (36 pages). The file includes a chart showing all Mitch's children with their living family members.

[68] *Eastern Cherokee Applications of the U.S. Court of Claims, 1906–1909*, microfilm publication M1104, 348 rolls (Washington, D.C.: National Archives Trust Fund Board, 1981), roll 308 (no. 39914, Dorothy Georgiana Bellenger, 26 August 1907; no. 39917, Tallula Alphretta Cook, 21 August 1907), roll 309 (no. 39959, Georgia C. House, 22 August 1907; nos. 970–73, Robert Philip House, Leonard Knoss House, Ollie House, William Evins House, 20–23 August 1907); roll 310 (nos. 40168–71, Paul C. Coker, Elizabeth Odessa Coker, Minerva Lula Saye, and Robert Earl Saye, 27–28 August 1907; nos. 40179–83, Ida A Adams, Lola Lee Daugherty, Susan A. Wells, Honor May Lee, and Maltha E. Johnson, 27–28 August 1907; no. 40186, Maggie Lee Fleming, Claud J. Jameson, Wm. P. Jameson, and Mae Miller, 26–27 August 1907; nos. 40235–37, George Columbus Covington, Georgia Elliot Covington, Bonner J. Covington, 24 August 1907; nos. 40240–45, Jamie Evins Fencher, Justinian Evins, Caroline Emma Martin, Minnie Dobbins, Frances Henrietta Lee, and Harry Newton Saye, 26 August 1907; and nos. 40247–49, Eugene Arthur Coker, Katie Covington Ansley, and Zeruah Naomi Garmon, 26 August 1907), roll 311 (no. 40252, Nancy Ramsey, 24 August 1907; no. 40255–57, Elizabeth Nancy Daniel, Mattie, Janie Robinson, and Georgia Belle Embry, 27 August 1907; and no. 40258, Ellen Eudora Owen, 24 August 1907), and roll 325 (no. 42417, Maggie L. Cook; and nos. 42419–23, Mary Lemma Coker, Jacqueline Jarrell, Fannie Emma Kemp, Charles D. Coker, and George Franklin Jarrell, 29 August 1909).

o John Evins, married a Miss Carter, a half Cherokee. John L. Evins was a son of this marriage. Among the eleven children of John L. Evins was Thomas M. Evins, a full brother of affiant.[69]

John L. Evins's grandchildren added further detail and family history:

o John Evin my Grand father was a soldier in the war of 1812 – he added the letter L to his his [sic] name after he settled here. he moved from Franklin Co. Ga. – and settled in the upper part of this, Fulton Co., about the year 1818 – where he lived all his after life and died at the old home in 1865 – John Evins father my great Grand Father was a welch man and lived in Virginia, he married a miss Carter who was a half breed Indian —so my Grand Father was a quarter breed Indian. — he was living in the county the year 1835 – at the same old house.[70]

o My father was born in Virginia. My grandfather came from Va. To Franklin Co., Ga., and my father came with him. … The Indian blood in our family came from the daughter of old man Carter. He married an Indian woman whose name I don't know, and had several daughters, one of whom was my grandmother.[71]

Both commissions denied all the Evins descendants' applications.

Conclusion

This study of Mitch's life from birth to death supports elements of his family's lore and suggests reasons for his departure. His repeated indebtedness combined with a large family likely motivated him to run away from his troubles. His family's violence, especially his brother's committing murder, might have contributed. He may have had Cherokee ancestry. Perhaps he really did throw his hat down, jump on it, and walk off.

---

[69] *Applications from the Bureau of Indian Affairs, Muskogee Area Office,* roll 37, application 2801, p. 31.

[70] *Eastern Cherokee Applications of the U.S. Court of Claims*, roll 310 (nos. 40235–36, George Columbus Covington and Georgia E. Covington, 24 August 1907). George likely quoted his mother, Georgia.

[71] Ibid., roll 308 (no. 39914, Dorothy Georgiana Bellenger, 26 August 1907). John C. Evins provided the testimony for Dorothy's application on 8 July 1908.

Chapter 11

Descendants of
Job Timberley and Rachel Melbourne[1]

Much of the development of family history along the south west coast of Newfoundland depends on the migration of families from the eastern part of Newfoundland along the coast toward the west. Many people have noted this general trend in family migration. And since much of this migration took place during the early years of settlement, there are certain times when few records show the movement of early families along the coast. Thus, it is difficult to trace the migration pathway for some early families, not because they didn't do what later families did, but because they did it early enough that the church was not established sufficiently to document their passing.

The Timberley[2] family of Burgeo and environs is a case in point. Job Timberley showed up in the records of the Burgeo Parish of the Church of England in the 1840s, resident at King's Harbour, Bay de Lieu,[3] and Burgeo. He had several children, many of whom appear in the Church records in either christenings or marriages (or both). The marriage of Job and Rachel is not documented there indicating that he might have been married when he arrived. Further, since Joseph H. Small states that Rachel was the daughter of "old grandmother Melbourne,"[4] not only is her surname probably Melbourne, but Job's migration to Burgeo was probably accompanied by others of his extended neighbors and family. Thus, Job's "appearance out of nothing" is only in accord with what we have come to believe about the settling of this part of Newfoundland.

Over the course of time, the Timberley family grew and dispersed as other families in this region have done. The available records are not complete and so this is a work still in progress. The structure of the first three generations of this family is as follows:

---

[1]   "Descendants of Job Timberley and Rachel Melbourne," *The Newfoundland Ancestor*, Vol 15, #3, Fall, 1999, pp 130-136.

[2]   Timberley is variously spelled Timbery, Timbry, Timbrey, Timberley, Timberly, Timburay, etc.

[3]   Variously spelled Bay du Lieu, Bay D;Leau, Bay de View, etc.

[4]   Joseph H. Small, "Diary of Burgeo, Newfoundland," transcription and extract of holograph original by Sydney Gordon Miles, *The Newfoundland Ancestor*, Vol. 13, #2, pp. 53-64; Vol. 13, #3, pp. 112-124; Vol. 13 #4, pp. 160-174; Vol. 14, #1, pp. 6-18. His reference to the Timberley family is in the final segment, pp. 78. Hereafter, references to this work will be to Small's Burgeo Diary.

Generation One

1. Job[1] Timberley, born about 1800[5] in England;[6] buried 22 January 1885 in Burgeo.[7] He married Rachel Melbourne,[8] buried 15 December 1863 in Lower Burgeo.[9]

Children of Job Timberley and Rachel Melbourne are as follows:

+   2   i.   Ann[2] Timberley, born 2 July 1842 in Bay de Lieu; christened 2 October 1842 in Bay de Lieu; died 2 December 1910 in Grey River; buried 5 December 1910 in Grey River. She married Thomas Lushman.

+   3   ii.   Jane[2] Timberley, born October 1845 in Bay de Lieu; died after 1921 in Burgeo. She married (1) George Strickland. She married (2) (---) Toms; and (3) (---) O'Brien.

+   4   iii.   Sarah[2] Timberley, born 6 March 1846 in Bay D'Leau; christened 11 April 1846 in Bay D'Leau. She married William Stickland.

+   5   iv.   James[2] Timberley, born about 1848; buried 30 November 1890 in Burgeo. He married Caroline Clark.

+   6   v.   George[2] Timberley. He married Jane (---).

     7   vi.   Charlotte[2] Timberley, christened 16 December 1855 in King's Harbour.[10]

     8   vii.   Edward[2] Timberley, christened 5 September 1858 in King's Harbour.[11]

Generation Two

2. Ann[2] Timberley (Job[1]), born 2 July 1842 in Bay de Lieu; christened 2 October 1842 in Bay de Lieu;[12] died 2 December 1910 in Grey River; buried 5 December 1910 in Grey

---

[5]   Calculated from age at burial.

[6]   Small's Burgeo Diary, Vol. 14, #1, p. 7.

[7]   Records of the Burgeo Parish, Church of England, *Burials, 1879-1912*, p. 9, line 1, #65, age 85 yr. Hereafter references to the Records of the Burgeo Parish will be by Parish Records and the title of the specific book.

[8]   It is not definitely known that Rachel's surname is Melbourne but is more likely than not.

[9]   Parish Recxords, *Baptisms, Marriages, and Burials 1855-1871*, p. 46, #77, no age given.

[10]   Parish Records, *Baptisms, Marriages, and Burials, 1855-1871*, p. 1, #18. Parents are listed as Job and Rachel Timbrery.

[11]   Parish Records, *Baptisms, Marriages, and Burials, 1855-1871*, p. 5, #110. Parents are listed as Job and Rachel Timbrery.

[12]   St John the Evangelist, Burgeo, NF, *Baptisms, Marriages, and Burials, 1842-1853*, p. 2, line 2, surname given is Timberland. FHL film 2,133,919, item 8, p 5, line 6, shows Ann Timberley, daughter of Job and Rachel Timberland, baptised at Bay de L'Eau, 2 October 1842 by Martin Blackmore.

River.[13] She married on 18 July 1867 in Lower Burgeo,[14] Thomas Lushman as his second wife,[15] born about 1829[16] in New Harbour. He was living at or near Burgeo in 1848[17] and at Fox Island in 1864.[18] He died after 1884[19] but before 1921,[20] son of Thomas Lushman and Susannah McDonald.

Child of Ann Timberley and Thomas Lushman:

9   i.   (---)3 Lushman, born aft 1867 in Little River.[21]

3. Jane2 Timberley (Job1), born October 1845 in Bay de Lieu;[22] died aft 1921 in Burgeo. She married first on 6 October 1863 in Lower Burgeo,[23] George Strickland, born about 1840;[24] buried 18 August 1870 in Bay de Lieu.[25] She married second (---) Toms. She married third (---) O'Brien.[26]

Children of Jane Timberley and George Strickland are as follows:

10   i.   Job3 Strickland, died 1900, unmarried, in Burgeo.[27]
11   ii.   (---)3 Strickland.

---

[13]   Parish Records, *Burials 1879-1912*, p. 96, #761, age 73. There are two Ann Lushman burials, this is the later of the two, with an age more consistent with her christening record.

[14]   Parish Records, *Baptisms, Marriages, and Burials, 1855-1871*, p. 38, #[131]. Surname given as Timbrey, he of Little River, she of Lower Burgeo. Small's Burgeo Diary, Vol. 14, #1, p. 7, states that he (Small) thought Ann married Thomas Lushman and had a son.

[15]   He was first married to Jane Hinks, 19 May 1864, at Little River, Parish Records, *Baptisms, Marriages, and Burials, 1855-1871*, p. 35, #[91].

[16]   *Reverend Martin Blackmore's Diary, 1845-1848*, transcription of a handwritten copy of the original, Queen Elizabeth II Library, Municipal University of Newfoundland, St. John's, following entry for 19 August 1845. In a confirmation list for that date (Lower Burgeo), Thomas is listed, age 16. He probably was single at that time.

[17]   *Report of the Newfoundland Church Society September, 1850*, St. John's, NF, J. W. M'Coubrey, 1850, p. xxxvi, shows him a donor of 5 sihllings, under the listing for Burgeo for 1848.

[18]   *Hutchinson's Newfoundland Directory, 1864-65*, under the listing for Fox Island with other families: John Anderson, James Bunter, B. Warren, Henry Warren, William Warren, and James Young.

[19]   He is mentioned in the account of the rescue of Howard Blackburn in January of 1883 and was present at a subsequent reunion with his lost brother, William, in the summer of the following year. See *Lone Voyager*, by Joseph E. Garland, Boston (MA): Little, Brown and Company, 1963, pp. 6-24.

[20]   He is not found in the 1921 Newfoundland Census for the Burgeo-Lapoile District.

[21]   Small's Burgeo Diary states that he thought the couple had a son, Vol. 14, #1, p. 7.

[22]   1921 Newfoundland Census, District of Burgeo and La Poile, p. 93, listed as Jane O'Brien.

[23]   Parish Records, *Baptisms, Marriages, and Burials, 1855-1871*, p. 33, #[84]. He is of Bay de Loup, she of White Bear Bay.

[24]   Calculated from age at burial.

[25]   Parish Records, *Baptisms, Marriages, and Burials, 1855-1871*, p. 48, #157. Age at death is 30 yr.

[26]   All three marriages are mentioned in Small's Burgeo Diary. Given names are not known for marriages 2 and 3.

[27]   Both children are mentioned in Small's Burgeo Diary, Vol. 14, #1, p. 7, but the second child was not named.

4. Sarah2 Timberley (Job1), born 6 March 1846 in Bay de Lieu; christened 11 April 1846 in Bay de Lieu.[28] She married on 28 August 1862 in Burgeo[29] William Stickland, born June 1825 in Rencontre West;[30] died about 1921.[31]

Children of Sarah Timberley and William Stickland are as follows:

12   i.   Rachel[3] Stickland, born March 1863 in West Point; died aft 1921.[32] She married Ephraim Matthews,[33] who died before 1921.

13   ii.   Edward3 Stickland.[34]

14   iii.   James3 Stickland. He married Mabel Crant, daughter of John Crant.[35]

15   iv.   John3 Stickland. He married Sarah Kinslow.[36]

16   v.   Joseph3 Stickland, died, unmarried, about 1910.[37]

+   17   vi.   Hannah3 Stickland, born April 1876 in Bay de Lieu; died aft 1921. She married George Sutton.

18   vii.   Charlotte3 Stickland, born 12 September 1883 in Bay de Lieu; christened 27 October 1883 in Bay de Lieu.[38]

19   viii. Sarah Maria3 Stickland, born 22 August 1886 in Bay de Lieu; christened 16 September 1886 in Bay de Lieu;[39] buried 15 December 1886 at Burgeo.[40]

5. James2 Timberley (Job1), born about 1848;[41] buried 30 November 1890 in Burgeo.[42] He married Caroline Clark,[43] christened 5 May 1863 in Squire's Cove, daughter of John Clark

---

[28]   Parish Records, *Baptisms, Marriages, and Burials, 1855-1871*, p. 9, #225. Parents are Job and Rachel Timburay.

[29]   Parish Records, *Baptisms, Marriages, and Burials, 1855-1871*, p. 33, #66. He is a widower, she a spinster, both are of King's Harbour.

[30]   1921 Newfoundland Census, District of Burgeo and La Poile, p. 95, gives birth month and year, age 96. It also lists Sarah Stickland, born Mar 1838, at Burgeo, age 83.

[31]   Small's Burgeo Diary, Vol. 14, #1, p. 7, states he died "five years ago," but he was alive in 1921 for the census.

[32]   1921 Newfoundland Census, District of Burgeo and La Poile, p. 98, Rachel Matthews. Ephraim not present with her.

[33]   Marriage mentioned in Small's Burgeo Diary, Vol. 14, #1, p. 7.

[34]   Mentioned in Small's Burgeo Diary, Vol. 14, #1, p. 7, probably died young.

[35]   Mentioned in Small's Burgeo Diary, Vol. 14, #1, p. 7. Not found in 1921 Newfoundland Census.

[36]   Mentioned in Small's Burgeo Diary, Vol. 14, #1, p. 7. Not found in 1921 Newfoundland Census.

[37]   Mentioned in Small's Burgeo Diary, Vol. 14, #1, p. 7.

[38]   Parish Records, *Baptisms, 1879-1893*, p. 33, #257. Parents are living at Bay de Loup.

[39]   Parish Records, *Baptisms, 1879-1893*, p. 50, #400. Parents are living at Bay de Loup.

[40]   Parish Records, *Burials, 1879-1912*, p. 16, #124. Buried at Burgeo.

[41]   Calculated from age at burial.

[42]   Parish Records, *Burials, 1879-1912*, p. 28, #217. James Timbrey.

[43]   Parents of Sarah Ellen Timbrey are listed as James and Caroline. Small's Burgeo Diary says that James Timberley married the daughter of "Mrs. Clarke."

and Susanna Lushman.[44]

Children of James Timberley and Caroline Clark are as follows:

+   20   i.   John3 Timberley. He married (---) Young.

+   21   ii.   William3 Timberley, born about 1878; died about 1903 in Burgeo. He married Rosannah Ingram.

      22   iii.   Sarah Ellen3 Timbrey, christened 10 April 1881 in Burgeo.[45]

      23   iv.   Isabella3 Timbury, born 15 August 1884 in Burgeo; christened 29 August 1884 in Burgeo;[46] buried 4 October 1884 in Burgeo.[47]

      24   v.   Isabella Clark3 Timbury, born 17 July 1887 in Burgeo; christened 12 August 1887 in Burgeo;[48] buried 24 March 1888 in Burgeo.[49]

      25   vi.   Susanna Litchman3 Timbury, christened 25 August 1889 in Burgeo.[50]

6. George2 Timberley (Job1). He married before 1864, Jane (---).[51]

Child of George Timberley and Jane (---) is as follows:

      26   i.   Mary Jane3 Timbry, christened 9 May 1864 in Bay de Lieu.[52]

Generation 3

17. Hannah3 Stickland (Sarah2 Timberley, Job1), born April 1876 in Bay de Lieu; died after

---

[44]   Parish Records, *Baptisms, Marriages, and Burials, 1855-1871*, p. 12, #280. Parents resident at Squire's Cove.

[45]   Parish Records, *Baptisms, 1879-1893*, p. 15, #119, parents are James and Caroline Timbrey, residence Burgeo.

[46]   Parish Records, *Baptisms, 1879-1893*, p. 37, #291, parents are James and Caroline Timbury, residence Burgeo.

[47]   Parish Records, *Burials, 1879-1912*, p. 8, #57. Age 6 weeks.

[48]   Parish Records, *Baptisms, 1879-1893*, p. 55, #438, parents are James and Caroline Timbury, residence Burgeo. The child's middle name supports the maiden name of her mother.

[49]   Parish Records, *Burials, 1879-1912*, p. 20, #160. Age 8 mo.

[50]   Parish Records, *Baptisms, 1879-1893*, p. 71, #561, parents are James and Caroline Timbury, residence Burgeo. The child's middle name supports the maiden name of her maternal grandmother and also reflects the experience with Howard Blackburn's rescue.

[51]   Named as father of Mary Jane Timbrery, George and Jane. If this is his first child, his age at marriage, if average, would place him as a possible child of Job Timberley. Only one family of that name has ever been mentioned in the records (of that time) or in Small's Burgeo Diary. There is no documentation to define him as a child of Job and Rachel Timberley.

[52]   Parish Records, *Baptisms, Marriages, and Burials, 1855-1871*, p. 14, #328. Parents George and Jane Timbrery, residence Bay de Loup.

1921.[53] She married George Sutton,[54] born July 1868 in Burgeo; died after 1921.[55]

Children of Hannah Stickland and George Sutton are as follows:

27 i. William4 Sutton. He married Millie Taylor.[56]
28 ii. John Wilson4 Sutton, born 19 December 1900 in Burgeo; christened 10 January 1901 in Burgeo.[57]
29 iii. Rachel Alice4 Sutton, born 8 October 1902 in Burgeo; christened 9 November 1902 in Burgeo.[58]
30 iv. Martha4 Sutton, born 20 April 1905 in Burgeo; christened 21 May 1905 in Burgeo.[59]
31 v. Jeremiah4 Sutton, born November 1908 in Louisburg, Nova Scotia, Canada.[60]
32 vi. Mary J.4 Sutton, born April 1910 in Burgeo.[61]
33 vii. Joseph4 Sutton, born November 1911 in Burgeo.[62]

20. John3 Timberley (James2, Job1), born about 1857.[63] He married before 1881 (---) Young.[64]

Child of John Timberley and (---) Young is as follows:

34 i. Sarah Ann4 Timberley, born about 1881. She married on 30 April 1903 in Burgeo,[65] Henry McDonald, born about 1879.

21. William3 Timberley (James2, Job1), born about 1878;[66] died about 1903 in Burgeo.[67] He

53   1921 Newfoundland Census, District of Burgeo and La Poile, p. 95.

54   Marriage mentioned in Small's Burgeo Diary, Vol. 14, #1, p. 7.

55   1921 Newfoundland Census, District of Burgeo and La Poile, p. 95.

56   Child and marriage mentioned in Small's Burgeo Diary, Vol. 14, #1, p. 7.

57   Parish Records, *Baptisms, 1893-1905*, p. 62, #493, parents are George and Mary Sutton, residence Burgeo. 1921 Newfoundland Census, District of Burgeo and La Poile, p. 95, daughter of George and Hannah.

58   Parish Records, *Baptisms, 1893-1905*, p. 77, #616, parents are George and Mary Sutton, residence Burgeo. 1921 Newfoundland Census, District of Burgeo and La Poile, p. 95, daughter of George and Hannah.

59   1921 Newfoundland Census, District of Burgeo and La Poile, p. 95, son of George and Hannah.

60   1921 Newfoundland Census, District of Burgeo and La Poile, p. 95, daughter of George and Hannah.

61   1921 Newfoundland Census, District of Burgeo and La Poile, p. 95, daughter of George and Hannah.

62   1921 Newfoundland Census, District of Burgeo and La Poile, p. 95, son of George and Hannah.

63   Assuming an average of 24 yrs for a male at marriage.

64   Mentioned in Small's Burgeo Diary, Vol. 14, #1, p. 7.

65   Parish Records, *Marriages, 1896=1906*, p. 44, #87, age 22, daughter of John, groom was 24. John signed as witness "John Timley."

66   Estimated from age at marriage and death.

67   Parish Records, *Burials, 1879-1912*, p. 72, #571, no date of death but place with others in September and October, 1903, died by drowning, age 25.

married on 27 December 1900 in Burgeo,[68] Rosannah Ingram, born about 1876; died 28 November 1904 in Burgeo; buried 29 November 1904 in Burgeo.[69]

Child of William Timberley and Rosannah Ingram is as follows:

35   i.   Mary Jane[4] Timberley, born 9 September 1901 in Burgeo; christened 28 September 1901 in Burgeo.[70]

---

[68]   Parish Records, *Marriages, 1896-1906*, p. 27, #53, groom age 22, son of James. Bride was 24, daughter of James.

[69]   Parish Records, *Burials, 1879-1912*, p. 77, #610, age 28 yrs.

[70]   Parish Records, *Baptisms 1893*-1905. 1921 Newfoundland Census, p. 88, living on Red Island, b September 1901.

Chapter 12

Shaving with Occam's Razor:
A Proposed Descendancy for Edward Warren
of Fox Island, Newfoundland[1]

Introduction

Occam's Razor is a scientific or philosophical principal which states that, other things being equal, the simplest explanation is most likely the correct one. Despite the many variations in human behavior, this proposition can effectively be used as a starting-place in constructing families for which there is absent or conflicting evidence. An example is the Warren family of Fox Island, Newfoundland, who lived in a small, isolated community for many years.

Tiny Fox Island is found just off the south coast of Newfoundland between White Bear Bay and Bay de Vieux, about 3 miles north-north-east of the eastern-most island of the Ramea group; the nearest larger mainland communities are Burgeo and Little River (now Grey River). Fishermen and their families settled on Fox Island possibly as early as 1818, and their descendants stayed as long as the fishing was good. At no time was this large community (the peak recorded population was 134 in 1911), but both a school and church were built there between 1877 and 1884.[2] Officially renamed Bonald's Island sometime between 1945 and 1956, the island has been abandoned since 1956.

The Warren family project began as an apparently unrelated collection of evidence,

---

[1]   "Shaving with Occam's Razor: A Proposed Descendancy for Edward Warren of Fox Island, Newfoundland," *The Newfoundland Ancestor*, Part 1, Vol 17, #4, Fall 2001, pp 185-194; Part 2, Vol 18, #1, Winter, 2002, pp 35-44; Part 3, Vol 18, #2, Spring, 2002, pp 65-74.

[2]   Joseph R. Smallwood, *The Newfoundland Encyclopedia*, St. John's (NF): Newfoundland Book Publishers, Ltd., 1967, article on Fox Island. On-line copy available at: <http://enl.cuff.com>.

found in the Burgeo and Ramea parish records;[3] three Newfoundland directories,[4] two diaries,[5] the 1921 and 1935 Newfoundland censuses for the Burgeo and La Poile District,[6] and the civil vital records of Newfoundland.[7]

This collection of data was presented to a seminar on evidence and analysis as an exercise in logic.[8] The assignment was to create a genealogical solution (one or more families) which incorporated all of the data in the collection.

The evidence is sparse for the first years of residence in the area, partly because Rev. Blackmore, the first permanent cleric in the area, didn't arrive in Burgeo until 1842. The family structure presented here is not the only one which could be constructed from the evidence, particularly in the third generation; there is not enough available evidence to conclusively define the whole family. However, using the principle of Occam's Razor, this is a logical family construction and a good point of beginning.

There are 49 individuals in the first three generations of this family, 26 of whom declare their parents by name either in their baptism record or their marriage record. The remaining 23 have no indication in the records of who their parents might be. We can single out reasons for one father to be assigned to 16 of these. The remaining 7 are arbitrarily assigned and provide the leaven to this loaf!

It may be helpful to refer to the chart of child-bearing years, Table 1, for the Warren family members discussed herein. The dashed lines indicate the approximate years during which a child may be attributed to him or her running from the marriage year to the death of the individual, spouse, or the wife reaching age 44.

Proposed descendants of Edward Warren (c1788-c1850)

---

[3]   Several Burgeo Parish books dating from 1842 containing baptisms, marriages, and burials, Parish records of the Burgeo Parish, Church of England, Burgeo, Newfoundland, Canada, *Baptisms, Marriages, Deaths, 1842-1855*; *Baptisms, Marriages, Deaths, 1855-1872*; *Baptisms 1879-1893*; *Marriages 1879-1896' Deaths 1879-1912*; *Baptisms 1893-1905*; *Marriages 1896-1906*; and *Baptisms 1917-1943*. hereafter referred to by their titles.

[4]   *Hutchinson's Newfoundland Directory for 1864-1865*, *McAlpine Newfoundland Directory for 1898*, and *McAlpine Newfoundland Directory for 1904*. All are available on-line at <**http://www.chebucto.org/Heritage/NGB**> (The Newfoundland Grand Banks site).

[5]   [Edward Wix], *Six Months of a Newfoundland Missionary's Journal, from February to August, 1835*, London: Smith, Elder and Co., 1836, and Martin Blackmore, *Rev. Martin Blackmore's Journal, 1845-48*, copy of hand-written transcription obtained from Queen Elizabeth Library, Memorial University of Newfoundland, St. John's, Newfoundland.

[6]   Newfoundland census for 1921, Burgeo-Lapoile District, National Archives of Canada microfilm reel M-8037, now available on microfilm from the Family History Library. Hereafter referred to as "NF Census 1921." Newfoundland census for 1935, Burgeo-Lapoile District, National Archives of Canada microfilm reel M-8048, hereafter referred to as "NF Census 1935."

[7]   Vital Records of Newfoundland held by the Provincial Archives of Newfoundland and Labrador, St. John's, Newfoundland, Births 1891-1902, Marriages 1891-1923, and Deaths 1891-1949, filmed by the Family History Library. Hereafter referred to as "Vital Records of NF."

[8]   William M. Litchman, "Teaching Analysis, Logic, and the Research Process: A Seminar Approach," *NGS Newsmagazine*, November/December, 2000, Vol. 26, #6, pp. 340-343.

First Generation

1. Edward Warren was born about 1788. He died between 1849 and 1852 in Fox Island. Among the earliest parish records are some Warren marriages in the Burgeo parish, which includes Fox Island: three marriages in 1844, one in July and two in September. The two September weddings (on the same day) were witnessed by Edward Warren. He was not a witness at the July wedding, perhaps because he was away fishing at that time. There are two further Warren weddings in 1849, both on the same day in September of that year, one witnessed by Edward Warren and the other by William Warren. Both of these weddings take place at the "house of Edward Warren at Fox Island." Edward does not appear on any record after this 1849 wedding and so he may have died soon thereafter. Except for that, he probably would have appeared as a witness at the September wedding of Grace Warren in 1852. There is a wedding in 1858 and two in 1862. The last two are both for men named Edward Warren.

Edward Warren could be 1) one individual or 2) two individuals. Of these two possibilities, one individual is simpler. He could be 1) related by blood or 2) not related by blood to other Warrens. A blood relationship is far more likely. He could have 1) the same relationship to all since they (the brides and grooms) are of the same generation. If only one relationship exists, he could be 1) father or uncle (i.e. one generation older) or 2) sibling or cousin (i.e. the same generation). Of these, the simplest is that he is their father.

The possibility of more than one wife for Edward is raised at this point only because there is one fairly wide gap (1813-1819) in the estimated birth years for these eight children indicating the possibility of the death of an earlier spouse and replacement by another. Neither of these women are named anywhere to answer this question. It is also possible that one or more children born in this interim period either died, married, and/or moved at some point and so don't appear in the later church records. Another argument is that the estimated ages for the children (and therefore birth years) are inaccurate and spread in a different fashion so that there really isn't any gap at all. It is probably simpler to assume one mother for all of these children with some children lost at young ages (creating the apparent gap).

Trying to construct this family using two early male parents (i.e. Edward and one other) produces many more complications. If there were two Warren men living at Fox Island early on, the second individual is *never* mentioned in any record. Since one parent can account for all of the known second generation Warren family members without difficulty it seems simplest to propose one male Warren parent, not two.

One bit of evidence supporting this conclusion comes from comments made by Rev. Blackmore in his diary. He lists results of an 1845 census of the district of Fortune Bay extending from Bonne Bay to Cape Ray. In this listing, he notes that there are only 13 families living in Fox Island, with 40 children and 63 individuals.[9] The families who are likely present at Fox Island in 1845 include William and Ann (Thornhill) Warren, John and Frances (Bonnell) Warren, Benjamin and Mary Hayman,

---

[9]   If the total number of single adults at Fox Island is x and all of these singles are counted as families, then the rest of the families, $13 - x$, must be couples. Thus, the total number of adults, $63 - 40 = 23$, must equal the sum of the singles plus twice the number of couples, i.e. $2(13 - x) + x = 23$, where x, the number of singles, can only be $= 3$.

Table 1.
Chart of child-bearing years for Warren family members:

Listed in order of appearance

```
              1810   1820   1830   1840   1850   1860   1870   1880   1890   1900   1910
              |--------|---------|---------|---------|---------|---------|---------|---------|---------|---------|


First Generation
Edward                    (-----------------------)        [1813-1837]

Second Generation
William [1837-1860]                       (-----|-------------)
John          [1844-49, 1856-79]       (-----)    (------------------)
Elizabeth (Osmond) [1844-67]           (--------------------)
Bavillam      [1849-1871]                 (----------------------)
Henry         [1849-1872]                 (-----------------------)
Grace (Melbourne)   [1852-75]                (----------------------)
Thomas [1858-62]                                     (---)
Edward  [1862-85]                                   (--------------------)

Third Generation
Edward  [1862-1862]                                  ()
Henry          [1871-91]                                 (------------------)
William [1862-85]                                   (--------------------)
Sarah (Clarke)      [1860-83]                       (--------------------)
Emma (McDonald)    [1884-19??]                                  (-----------------------)
Susannah (Bagg) [1894-19??]                                         (--------------)
John            [1892-96]                                      (---)
James (Susannah Warren) [1881-1908]                          (-----------------------)
Ann (Vardy)        [1886-1903]                              (-----------------)
Thomas [1882-1886]                                          (---)
George           [1901-19??]                                            (------)
Elizabeth (Cole) [1865-88]                          (-------------------------)
Thomas [1879-1902]                                         (----------------------)
William [1880-1903]                                        (----------------------)
Edward [1879-91]                                           (-----------)
Henry           [1881-93]                                  (------------)
Hannah (Matthews)    [1879-98]                            (-----------------)
Susannah (James Warren) [1881-1908]                       (--------------------------)
Elizabeth (Edward Wm Warren)  [1887-96]                           (-----)
Albert John       [1879-1902]                             (---------------------)
Isabella (Bungay)  [1886-90]                                      (---)
Edward William (Elizabeth Warren) [1887-96]                       (-----)
Thomas [1880-92]                                          (----------)
```

James and Elizabeth Young, William and Mary Kettle, Kish and Esther Cains, John and Elizabeth (Warren) Osmond, James Bunter and wife, the parents of Ann Thornhill, and the parents of Frances Bonnell, ten couples, plus Edward Warren (assuming he is a widower by this time), Thoms Lushman,[10] and Edward Trick, three possible singles.[11]

From this evidence, Edward must have been born about 1788 (based on the birth year for his eldest proposed child)[12] and died about 1849-52. If his wife was born about 1792, her fertile years could cover the years 1813 through 1836 (age 44). Edward and his wife have the following children:

+	2	i.	William Warren was born ca 1813.
+	3	ii.	John Warren was born ca 1819.
	4	iii.	Elizabeth Warren was born about 1822. Elizabeth married John Osmond on 13 July 1844 in Fox Island.[13] John was born about 1820.
+	5	iv.	Bavillam Warren was born ca 1824.
+	6	v.	Henry Warren was born ca 1830.
+	7	vi.	Grace Warren was born ca 1833.
+	8	vii.	Thomas Warren was born ca 1833.
+	9	viii.	Edward Warren was born ca 1837.

Second Generation

2. William Warren (Edward) was born ca 1813. He was buried on 12 November 1891 in Tibbo's Cove.[14] William married first Grace. Grace was born ca 1816.

Grace, first child of William and Grace, was born ca 1837 and baptised on the same

[10]   *Report of the Newfoundland Church Society, September, 1850*, St. John's (NF): J. W. M'Coubrey, Printer, 1850, Appendix, Subscribers, p. XXXVI, listed with "Burgeo." A microfilm version of this publication is available from the Canadian Institute of Historical Manuscripts, No. 39997 (ISBN 0-665-39997-9).

[11]   These names are gleaned from the Parish records of the Burgeo Parish, as being residents of Fox Island at or before 1845: *Baptisms, Marriages, Burials, 1842-1855* (Baptisms and Marriages).

[12]   In a study of marriages of 195 spinsters and 186 bachelors from the Burgeo parish records, it was found that the average for bachelors over the period 1842-1900 was 25.3 years and that for spinsters was 21.8 years. The average difference in age between bachelor and spinster is 3.5 years. This average was determined by finding the difference in marriage age for all bachelor/spinster marriages rather than finding the difference between the average marriage ages only. The total range of marriage ages for bachelors ran from 18 to 51 years and for spinsters from 15 to 45 years. Parish records of the Burgeo Parish, Church of England, Burgeo, Newfoundland, Canada. All estimated birth years are based on these averages unless otherwise noted.

[13]   Elizabeth is born too early to be a daughter of William so must be a child of Edward. *Baptisms, Marriages, Deaths, 1842-1855*. (Marriages) p. 4, #12, witness Edward Pink.

[14]   *Hutchinson's Newfoundland Directory for 1864-1865* shows B. Warren, Henry Warren, and William Warren in Fox Island. *Lovell's Canadian Dominion Newfoundland Directory for 1871*, vol. 8 (Newfoundland), Montreal: John Lovell, 1871, shows John Warren, William Warren, sr, and William Warren, jr. *Deaths, 1879-1912*, p. 30, #235, age 78. Vital Records of NF, FHL film 2,168,429, Death Bk No. 1, p. 53, #38, gives date 11 November 1891, and age as 48 (mis-reading of 78)

day that William Warren (her father) and Ann Thornhill (*bachelor* and spinster of Fox Island) were married. The implication of the bachelor note is that there must be two Williams. The simplest theory is to have only one William (son of Edward) with two wives in sequence, even in the face of the "bachelor" declaration for his second marriage. Secondly, the baptism of a child of William and Grace on the same day and place as the marriage of William and Ann only sounds reasonable with one William. William Warren was known to be in Fox Island in 1831.[15]

There are three other children born early enough to qualify as children of William and Grace; all born prior to the marriage of William and Ann or the marriage of any of his siblings. Edward already has living children of these names. The children could be named Grace (for the mother), Edward (for the paternal grandfather), William (for the father) and Henry (possibly for the maternal grandfather.

William and Grace have the following children:

	10	i.	Grace Warren was born 24 May 1837 in Fox Island and was christened 9 September 1844 in Fox Island.[16]
	11	ii.	Edward Warren was born ca 1837. He married Maria Young.[17]
+	12	iii.	Henry Warren was born ca 1840.
+	13	iv.	William Warren was born ca 1841.

William married second Ann Thornhill 9 September 1844 in Fox Island.[18] Ann was born ca 1823.

3. John Warren (Edward) was born ca 1819 in Fox Island.[19] John married first Frances Bonnell 9 September 1844 in Fox Island.[20] Frances was born ca 1827. She died 9 May 1849 in Fox Island.[21]

Sarah Warren (born ca 1849), has no parent declared and could have been the daughter of John, Bavillam, or Henry. Bavillam cannot be her father since he named another child Sarah. Henry has another child born in March 1850. Sarah has been assigned to John

[15]   Joseph R. Smallwood, *The Newfoundland Encyclopedia*, St. John's (NF): Newfoundland Book Publishers, Ltd., 1967, article on Fox Island states: "According to Donale Crewe (1976), James and Mitchel Strickland left Fox Island to settle nearby Deer Island in the 1830s. William Warren and Benjamin Haymen were listed as residents of Fox Island in 1831 and 1840, respectively, and James Young was repoted to be a fisherman of Fox Island in 1844..."

[16]   *Baptisms, Marriages, Deathc, 1842-1855*, (Baptisms) p. 5, #140, daughter of William and Grace Warren.

[17]   William M. Litchman, "Descendants of James Young and Elizabeth (---)," *The Newfoundland Ancestor*, Vol. 16, #2, Summer 2000, pp. 64-74.

[18]   *Baptisms, Marriages, Deaths, 1842-1855*, (Marriages) p. 5, #17, William is bachelor, witnesses Edward Warren and Kish Cains.

[19]   *Lovell's Canadian Dominion Newfoundland Directory for 1871*, vol. 8 (Newfoundland), Montreal: John Lovell, 1871, shows John Warren, William Warren, sr, and William Warren, jr. John is a son of Edward because of his time of birth. Died after 1865.

[20]   *Baptisms, Marriages, Deaths, 1842-1855*, (Marriages) p. 4, #16, witnesses Edward Warren and Kish Cains.

[21]   *Baptisms, Marriages, Deaths, 1842-1855*, (Burial) p. 18, #51.

and Frances.

   After Frances died, five other children designated as children of "John Warren" were born. There are also two further children, probably twins, who have their parents declared as John and Elizabeth. This means that John must have married again after Frances' death but before the birth of the first of the second group of children (estimated to be ca 1856).

   There is one child, Thomas, who married a woman named Elizabeth and had three children designated as children of Thomas and Elizabeth. This Thomas is different from Thomas (b ca 1855) who married Mary Ann; and Thomas (b ca 1869), the son of Edward and Jane who married Elizabeth Ann Clarke. This Thomas, by the date of his birth, could be the son of John, Bavillam, Edward, Henry, or William. Henry has a child whose birth date conflicts with that of this Thomas, and Bavillam, Edward and William all have children by the name of Thomas. The only man left is John who, with his wife, Elizabeth, could be the parents of this Thomas.

   Henry Warren, born ca 1858, is a candidate to be a child of John, Bavillam, Henry, or Thomas. Henry already has a son named Henry and another child born in that year so he is highly unlikely as a father. William and Albert John are also born in 1858 and with Henry, these three must be assigned to those three fathers. Only Albert John survives to the 1921 Newfoundland census and he is found living alone as a widower in Fox Island, giving no indication as to his sibling(s). These are three of the seven *arbitrary* assignments to parents. Henry is assigned to John, William to Bavillam, and Albert John to Thomas.

   Two more children, suggested by later marriage records to have been born in the late 1850s do not appear in any of the earlier records. Mary Jane Warren married Ezekiel McDonald in 1880, giving her a birth year of ca 1859, and after her death, he married Emma Warren in 1884. Ezekiel and Emma are alive in 1921 where we find Emma's birth to be February 1859 in Fox Island. The fact that these two Warren women from Fox Island both married the same man suggests that they might have been sisters (or at least closely related) and the closeness of their supposed birth dates suggests that they might, in fact, be twin sisters. John, Bavillam, Henry, or Thomas may be their father and there is not much to tell us which is more likely. However, John already has two sets of twins in his family which is encouraging. These two women are assigned to John and Elizabeth since this seems to be the simplest construction based on the slim evidence remaining.

\   John and Frances have the following children:

14   i.   Rebecca Warren was born 5 June 1845 in Fox Island and was christened on 5 September 1845 in Fox Island.[22]
15   ii. Sarah Warren was born ca 1849. She married Francis Clarke.[23]

John married second Elizabeth. Elizabeth was born ca 1836. She died 21 April 1899

[22] *Baptisms, Marriages, Deaths, 1842-1855*, (Baptisms) p. 12, #312, daughter of John and Frances Warren.
[23] William M. Litchman, "Descendants of John Clarke and Susanna Lushman," *The Newfoundland Ancestor*, Vol. 16, #1, Spring 2000, pp. 22-28.

110

in Fox Island and was buried 24 April 1899 in Fox Island.[24]

If John married Elizabeth in 1856, she would have been about 20 years old at that time, nearly the average age at marriage for spinster women. There is no other known Warren man of this time for whom she would qualify as a widow and so the simplest conclusion is that she is the second wife of John Warren and the mother of those twelve children. Elizabeth Warren is named widow of John.[25]

John and Elizabeth have the following children:

	16	iii.	Henry Warren was born ca 1858. He married Elizabeth Louisa Rose on 14 September 1882 in Burgeo.[26]
	17	iv.	Mary Jane Warren was born ca 1859. She married Ezekiel McDonald 13 September 1880 in Fox Island.[27]
+	18	v.	Emma Warren was born February 1859.
+	19	vi.	Susannah Warren was born ca 1860.
+	20	vii.	John Warren was born ca 1861.
+	21	viii.	James Warren was born August 1861.
+	22	ix.	Thomas Warren was born June 1863 at Little River.
+	23	x.	Ann Warren was born 28 May 1864 at Little River.
	24	xi.	Frances Warren was born 7 September 1865 in Little River.[28] Frances married Francis Lushman 21 May 1889 in Little River[29] as his second wife.[30] Francis was born ca 1859 in Little River.
	25	xii.	Barzillai Warren was christened 21 October 1868 in Fox Island.[31]
	26	xiii.	Mary Rebecca Warren was christened 21 October 1868 in Fox Island.[32]
+	27	xiv.	George Warren was born May 1875.

5. Bavillam Warren (Edward) was born ca 1824 in Fox Island. He died on 22 December 1896

---

[24] *Burials 1879-1912*, p. 55 #435, widow, age 63 yrs. Vital Records of NF, FHL film 2,268,727, Death Bk No. 3, p. 374, #5.

[25] *McAlpine Newfoundland Directory for 1898*, entry for Fox Island.

[26] Parish records of the Burgeo Parish, on-line edition, <http://www.chebucto.com/NGB>.

[27] *Marriages 1879-1896*, p [8c], # [16c].

[28] Source: <http://www.chebucto.ns.ca/Heritage/NGB/Parish/>, Fortune – Belleoram, Church of England Baptisms 1846-1866, downloaded copy in possession of the author, states christening was at Facheau.

[29] *Marriages 1879-1896*, p. 66, #114, the daughter of John Warren.

[30] *Marriages 1879-1896*, p. 15, #30, the son of Thomas.

[31] *Baptisms, Marriages, Burials, 1855-1872*, (Baptisms) p. 23, #547, the son of John and Elizabeth Warren.

[32] *Baptisms, Marriages, Burials, 1855-1872*, (Baptisms) p. 23, #548, the daughter of John and Elizabeth Warren.

in Coppett and was buried 24 December 1896 in Coppett.[33] Bavillam married Susan Hayman 21 September 1849 in Fox Island.[34] Susan was born ca 1827.

The church records have only one documented child for Bavillam and Susan (Hayman) Warren (born 1863) after a marriage beginning in 1849. Thus, there could easily be a number of children born to this couple, some of whom may have died, leaving no record. Thomas is one such or possibly Edward (both born ca 1855). They could also be assigned to Henry but probably not both to the same father unless our estimated birth years are wrong, or they are twins. Thomas has arbitrarily been assigned to Bavillam. These are another two (making five so far) of the seven totally arbitrary assignments.

Elizabeth can only have been the daughter of either Bavillam or Henry. Since Henry later has a child by the name of Elizabeth (born 1870) her father is almost certainly Bavillam.

Bavillam and Susan have the following children:

+   28 i.   Elizabeth Warren was born March 1850.
     29 ii.   Benjamin Warren was born ca 1853.[35] Benjamin married Margarate Belle MacDonald, daughter of John and Catherine MacDonald, 16 September 1885, at Ingonish, Nova Scotia, Canada.[36]
     30 iii. Thomas Warren was born ca 1855.
     31 iv.   William Warren was born about 1858.
     32 v.   Samuel Warren was born 21 November 1860 in Fox Island and was christened in Fox Island.[37] He died 13 June 1945 and was buried 15 June 1945 in Neil's Harbour, Victoria, Nova Scotia.[38]
     33 vi.   Sarah Warren was christened 7 July 1863 in Fox Island.[39] Sarah

---

[33]   *Hutchinson's Newfoundland Directory for 1864-1865* shows B. Warren, Henry Warren, and William Warren in Fox Island. *Burials, 1879-1912*, p. 44, #351. Vital Records of NF, FHL film 2,168,729, p. 227, #31, died and buried at Coppett, age 72.

[34]   *Baptisms, Marriages, Burials, 1842-1854*, (Marriages) p. 13, #50, witnesses are John Jordan and William Warren.

[35]   Found in the 1881 Canadian census for Cape North, FHL film 1,37,802, p. 20, line 21, listed with the Abraham Hayman family, age 27. Also found with the same family in the 1871 Canadian census, FHL film 0,493,612, Ingonish, Victoria county, Nova Scotia, District #204, p. 16, line 19, age 18.

[36]   Marriage Records of Victoria County, Nova Scotia, Canada, Vol. 522, #31, FHL film 1,316,438, item 2.

[37]   Vital Records of NF, FHL film 2,132,977, delayed birth registrations, amongst retakes at first of film, gives parents as Barzillai and Susan Warren. 1901 Canadian census for Neil's Harbour, Victoria county, Nova Scotia, shows Samuel as a single domestic in the houshold of Abram and Mary Hayman, all immigrated to NS in 1869, FHL film 1,843,538, age 40. He is also found with the same family in the 1891 Canadian census for New Haven (close by Neil's Harbour), FHL film 1,464,746, p. 9, line 9, age 30, and the 1881 Canadian census with the same family at Cape North, FHL film 1,375,802, p. 20, line 22, age 20. He was not presnet with the family as listed in the 1871 Canadian census, FHL film 0,493,612.

[38]   Death register is found in the parish records for St. Andrew's Anglican Church, Niel's Harbour, film 11,693x.

[39]   *Baptisms, Marriages, Burials, 1855-1872*, (Baptisms) p. 13, #299, the daughter of Barzillai and Susannah Warren.

married George Bowles 13 September 1883 in Fox Island.[40]
George was born ca 1859 in Coppett.[41]

6. Henry Warren was born ca 1824 in Fox Island.[42] Henry married Elizabeth Hayman 21 September 1849 in Fox Island.[43] Elizabeth was born ca 1832. She died 6 December 1914 in Fox Island.[44]
 Henry and Elizabeth have the following children:

34	i.	Edward Warren was born ca 1855.
35	ii.	Henry Warren was born ca 1856. He married Susannah Bowles.[45]
36	iii.	Hannah Warren was born ca 1858.
37	iv.	Benjamin Warren was christened 5 May 1863 in Fox Island.[46]
38	v.	Jane Warren was christened 21 September 1864 in Fox Island.[47]
39	vi.	Susanna Warren was christened 25 July 1867
40	vii.	Elizabeth Warren was christened 20 May 1870.

7. Grace Warren (Edward) was born ca 1830 in Fox Island. Grace married James Melbourne on 22 September 1852.[48] James was born ca 1828.
 James and Grace have the following children:

41	i.	William Melbourne was christened 4 November 1855 in Furby's Island.[49]
42	ii.	James Melbourne was christened 6 January 1859 in King's

---

[40] *Marriages 1879-1896*, p. 28, #[47a].

[41] William M. Litchman, "Descendants of Henry Bowles and Bridget Lushman," *The Newfoundland Ancestor*, Vol. 15, #4, Winter 1999, pp. 225-230.

[42] *Hutchinson's Newfoundland Directory for 1864-1865* shows B. Warren, Henry Warren, and William Warren in Fox Island. Died after 1870 but before 1898 (wife is listed in *McAlpine Newfoundland Directory for 1898*, entry for Fox Island, as Elizabeth, widow of Henry).

[43] *Baptisms, Marriages, Burials, 1842-1855*, (Marriages) p. 13, #49, witnesses are John Jordan and Edward Warren.

[44] *Burials, 1879-1912*, p. 55, #435. Vital Records of NF, FHL film 2,168,729, Death Book No. 6, p. 412, #25, of senility, age 82.

[45] William M. Litchman, "Descendants of Henry Bowles and Bridget Lushman," *The Newfoundland Ancestor*, Vol. 15, #4, Winter 1999, pp. 225-230. Additional information not found in this publication: their son, Henry William Warren, died in October 1919 in Fox Island; their son Charles Warren died on 3 March 1903 in Fox Island and was buried on 6 March 1903 in Fox Island; their son George Francis Warren was born 7 August 1893 in Fox Island and married Mary before 1921.

[46] *Baptisms, Marriages, Burials, 1855-1872*, (Baptisms) p. 12, #283, the son of Henry and Elizabeth Warren.

[47] *Baptisms, Marriages, Burials, 1855-1872*, (Baptisms) p. 17, #391, the daughter of Henry and Elizabeth Warren.

[48] *Baptisms, Marriages, Burials, 1842-1855*, (Marriages) p. 6, #61, witnesses are Job Timburley and Eliz. Bunter. Grace is a spinster of King's Harbour, James a bachelor of Bay de Loup.

[49] *Baptisms, Marriages, Burials, 1855-1872*, (Baptisms) p. 1, #14, the son of James and Grace.

Harbour.[50]

8. Thomas Warren (Edward) was born ca 1833 in Fox Island. He died in 1862.[51] Thomas married Sarah Hunt 13 September 1858 in Ramea.[52] Sarah was born ca 1837 in Ramea. Sarah Warren subsequently married John Meade in 1863[53] which is supportive of the early death proposed for Thomas.

Thomas and Sarah have the following children:

43   i.   Albert John Warren was born June 1858.

44   ii.   Isabella Warren was christened 3 June 1861.

9. Edward Warren (Edward) was born ca 1837 in Fox Island. He died before 1898.[54] Edward married Jane Rose 1 July 1862 in Ramea.[55] Jane was born ca 1844 in Fox Island. She died 21 April 1933 in Fox Island, age 89.[56]

There are two men of the second or third generation named Edward Warren. Both were born ca 1837 and both married in 1861. One died in 1862, age 25 years,[57] shortly after marrying Maria Young[58] (she subsequently married John Bagg in 1866 – as Maria Warren, widow[59]). The other one married Jane Rose.

Edward (husband of Jane) has been assigned as a child of Edward, and Edward (husband of Maria) to William, eldest son of Edward. There is no direct evidence which reveals the parents of these two contemporary Edwards but we know that they are not likely both children of the same father and there are no other Warren fathers of child siring condition available in 1837. These are the last two of the seven arbitrary lineage assignments.

James Warren (born August 1861, son of John) is found living in the same household with his aunt Jane Warren (widow) in 1921. The next listed household is that of Jane's son, Edward. Her age is given as 70 years in 1921 which would make her only 11 when she

---

50   *Baptisms, Marriages, Burials, 1855-1872*, (Baptisms) p. 6, #133, the son of James and Grace.

51   Death stated to be 1862 in Victor G. Kendall and Victor Kendall, *Ramea's Family Tree*, (Corner Brook, NF): Victor G. and Victor Kendall, 1995.

52   *Baptisms, Marriages, Burials, 1855-1872*, (Marriages) p. 30, #[36], the witnesses are Alfred Hunt and Christopher Dicks.

53   *Baptisms, Marriages, Burials, 1855-1872*, (Marriages) p. 34, #[77], she is a widow of Ramea, date 15 September 1863.

54   Died after 1870. *McAlpine Newfoundland Directory for 1898*, entry for Fox Island, shows Jane, widow of Edwaqrd and Edward, son of Edward.

55   *Baptisms, Marriages, Burials, 1855-1872*, (Marriages) p. 33, #[61].

56   NF Census 1921, lists Jane Warren, b 1851, living with nephew James (born August 1861) and next door to Edward (born May 1863). Her age is a bit young (by about 8-10 years). *McAlpine Newfoundland Directory for 1898*, entry for Fox Island, shows Jane, widow of Edwaqrd. *Baptisms, Marriages, Burials, 1855-1872*, (Marriages) p. 33, #[61]. Vital Records of NF, FHL film 2,168,731, Death Bk No. 11, p. 431, #39, born Fox Island, age 89 (born 1844).

57   *Baptisms, Marriages, Burials, 1855-1872*, (Burials) p. 46, #68.

58   *Baptisms, Marriages, Burials, 1855-1872*, (Marriages) p. 33, #[62].

59   *Baptisms, Marriages, Burials, 1855-1872*, (Marriages) p. 38, #[128].

married. Since James age is significantly young, hers may be as well. Her age at death is 89 years, a much more sensible age (born 1844).

Edward and Jane have the following children:

45 i.   Edward William Warren was christened 6 May 1863.
46 ii.   Barzillia Warren was christened 19 May 1864 in Coppett.[60]
47 iii. Rebecca Jane Warren was christened 19 September 1867 in Little River.[61]
48 iv.   Thomas Warren was christened 17 April 1869 in Little River.[62] He died 23 August 1893 in Fox Island.[63] Thomas married Elizabeth Ann Clarke, daughter of Francis Clark and Sarah Warren, 15 September 1892 in Fox Island.[64]
49 v.   Elizabeth Warren was born March 1872 in Little River.[65] Elizabeth married Samuel Cole(y) 6 September 1897 in Fox Island.[66] Samuel was born ca 1872 in Fox Island, the son of William Cole and Elizabeth Warren. See No. 94.

Third Generation[67]

12. Henry Warren (William, Edward) was born ca 1840 in Fox Island. He died 24 June 1910 in Burgeo and was buried on 26 June 1910 in Burgeo.[68] Henry married Frances Hayman 25 September 1871 in Fox Island.[69] Frances was born August 1849 in Fox Island. She died after

---

[60]   *Baptisms, Marriages, Burials, 1855-1872*, (Baptisms) p. 15, #338, the son of Edward and Jane Warren. NF Census 1921, p. 50, wife Mary J., born 1873.

[61]   *Baptisms, Marriages, Burials, 1855-1872*, (Baptisms) p. 22, #510, the daughter of Edward and Jane Warren.

[62]   *Baptisms, Marriages, Burials, 1855-1872*, (Baptisms) p. 24 #555, the son of Edward and Jane Warren.

[63]   Vital Records of NF, FHL film 2,168,994, Death Bk No. 2, p. 410, #13, "natural causes," age 25, bur Fox Island.

[64]   *Marriages, 1879-1896*, p. 95, #165, the son of Edward Warren. William M. Litchman, "Descendants of John Clarke and Susannah Lushman," *The Newfoundland Ancestor*, Vol. 16, #1, Spring 2000, pp. 22-28.

[65]   NF Census 1921, p. 56, Elizabeth Coley, born March 1874, age 47, living with Samuel (no children), living at Swyers Cove, born Little River.

[66]   Vital Records of NF, FHL film 2,168,995, Marriage Bk No. 3, p. 386, #11.

[67]   William M. Litchman, "Shaving with Occam's Razor: A Proposed Descendancy for Edward Warren of Fox Island, Newfoundland, Part II," *The Newfoundland Ancestor*, Part 2, Vol 18, #1, Winter, 2002, pp 35-44.

[68]   Victor G. Kendall and Victor Kendall, *Ramea's Family Tree*, (Corner Brook, NF): Victor G. and Victor Kendall, 1995, gives Henry's death date as 1903 (does not agree with Burgeo Parish records). *McAlpine Newfoundland Directory for 1898*, entry for Burgeo, shows Henry Warren living in Burgeo. *Burials, 1879-1912*, p. 94, #745. Vital Records of NF, FHL film 2,168,728, Death Bk No. 5, p. 402, line 28, age 70 years, born and buried Fox Island.

[69]   *Baptisms, Marriages, Burials, 1855-1872*, (Marriages) p. 43, #[187].

1921.[70]

Henry and Frances had the following children:

50 i. Mary Warren was born ca 1873 in Burgeo. Mary married John Anderson 5 October 1896 in Burgeo.[71] John was born ca 1873 in Burgeo.

51 ii. John Warren was born ca 1877 in Fox Island. John married Elizabeth Anderson 14 October 1898 in Burgeo.[72] Elizabeth died 12 June 1909 in Burgeo.[73]

52 iii. Benjamin Warren was christened 23 August 1880 in Fox Island.[74] Benjamin married Bertha Mary Hatcher 15 October 1910 at Burgeo.[75] Bertha was born 13 January 1890 and baptised 9 June 1890 in Ramea.[76]

53 iv. Thomas Warren was born 24 September 1881 and was christened 14 October 1881 in Fox Island.[77] Thomas married Julia E. (---) before 1919. Julia was born ca 1896.[78]

54 v. Joseph Henry Warren was born 24 January 1885 and was christened 25 January 1885 in Burgeo. He died 6 August 1961.[79]

---

[70] NF Census 1921, p. 109, widow, born August 1849 (Fox Island) living with Samuel and Agnes Warren. Victor G. Kendall and Victor Kendall, *Ramea's Family Tree*, (Corner Brook, NF): Victor G. and Victor Kendall, 1995, gives death date of 1891. This cannot be true because of her presence as a widow with the family of her son, Samuel, in 1921.

[71] *Marriages, 1879-1896*, p. 121, #217, the daughter of Henry Warren. Vital Records of NF, FHL film 2,168994, Marriage Bk No. 2, p. 481, #5.

[72] Mentioned in an email from Trudy Warren, 7 June 2000, that John is the son of Henry. Vital Records of NF, FHL film 2,168994, Marriage Bk No. 3, p. 389, #9, John Warren (21) and Elizabeth Anderson (20), 14 October 1898. Same marriage in church records gives date one year later. *Marriages, 1879-1896*, p. 12, #[23], 14 October 1899, groom son of Henry Warren, bride daughter of Eli Anderson.

[73] Vital Records of NF, FHL film 2,168,728, Death Bk No. 5, p. 400, #14, Elizabeth Warren, age 28, of TB at Burgeo (born c 1881).

[74] *Baptisms, Marriages, Burials, 1855-1872*, (Baptisms) p. 11, #86, the son of Henry and Fanny Warren, NF Census 1921, p. 67, born February 1879 (Fox Island), wife Bertha, born January 1889 (Ramea), children: Cyril, born January 1911 (Ramea), Geneve, born January 1915 (Ramea), Alva, born April 1917 (Ramea), and Israel, born March 1921 (Ramea). Mentioned in Victor G. Kendall and Victor Kendall, *Ramea's Family Tree*, (Corner Brook, NF): Victor G. and Victor Kendall, 1995, where it states that he married in 1910.

[75] Vital Records of NF, FHL film 2,168996, Marriage Bk No. 6, p. 386, #3, he was age 29, she 21.

[76] NF Census 1921, Ramea, p. 67. *Baptisms 1879-1893*, p. 75, #600.

[77] *Baptisms, 1879-1893*, p. 21, #164, the son of Henry and Frances Warren. NF Census 1921, p. 107, born September 1883 (Fox Island), wife Julia E., born December 1895 (Rose Blanche), child: Nina, born October 1908 (Burgeo). Mentioned in Victor G. Kendall and Victor Kendall, *Ramea's Family Tree*, (Corner Brook, NF): Victor G. and Victor Kendall, 1995.

[78] NF Census 1935, p. 494.

[79] *Baptisms, 1879-1893*, p. 40, #317, the son of Henry and Fanny Warren. NF Census 1921, p. 108, born February 1882 (Burgeo), wife, Harriett, born October 1890 (Burgeo), children: Hazel, born May 1910 (Burgeo), Chrissy, born May 1912 (Burgeo), Joseph, born January 1917 (Burgeo), Edgar, born May 1919 (Burgeo), and Ellen, born August 1921 (Burgeo).

Joseph married Harriet Jane Benoit 18 September 1907 at Burgeo.[80] Harriet was born ca 1890 in Gable Pond. She died 28 January 1974.[81]

55 vi. Samuel Warren was born 4 April 1888 and was christened on 26 April 1888 in Burgeo.[82] Samuel married first Elizabeth Ingraham 16 February 1913 in Burgeo.[83] Elizabeth was born ca 1883 in Burgeo. She died 18 January 1917 at Burgeo.[84] He married second Agnes Benoite 26 November 1917 at Burgeo.[85]

56 vii. Amy Warren was born 11 July 1893 and christened 25 August 1893 in Burgeo.[86]

13. William Warren (William, Edward) was born ca 1841 in Fox Island.[87] William married Frances Rose 1 July 1862 in Fox Island.[88] Frances was born ca 1845. She died 11 October 1927 in Burgeo.[89]

William and Frances have the following children:

57 i. Thomas William Warren was born ca 1862 in Cape la Hune. Thomas married Ann Barter 5 September 1889 in Cape la Hune.[90] Ann was born ca 1859 in Cape la Hune.

58 ii. John Henry Warren was christened 19 May 1864 in Fox Island.[91] John married Mary Ann Young 16 July 1886 in Little River.[92] Mary was born ca 1869 in Little River.

59 iii. Rebecca Warren was christened 30 August 1866 in Fox Island.[93]

60 iv. Elizabeth Jane Warren was christened 21 October 1868 in Fox

---

[80] Vital Records of NF, FHL film 2,168996, Mariage Bk No. 5, p. 382, #14.

[81] Trudy Warren, email of 2 June 2000 in possession of the author.

[82] *Baptisms, 1879-1893*, p. 40, #317, the son of Henry and Fanny Warren. NF Census 1921, p. 109, born April 1886 (Burgeo), wife, Agnes, born August 1897 (Burgeo), child: Myrtle, born April 1921 (Burgeo). Also widow, Frances Warren, born August 1849 (Fox Island).

[83] Vital Records of NF, FHL film 2,168,997, Marriage Bk No. 7, p. 382, #11.

[84] Vital Records of NF, FHL film 2,168,729, Death Bk No. 7, p. 398, age 23 yrs.

[85] Vital Records of NF, FHL film, 2,168,997, Marriage Bk No. 8, p 396, #5.

[86] Vital Records of NF, FHL film, 2,168,998, Birth Bk No. 2, p. 274, #1. *Baptisms, 1893-1906*, p. 1, #4, the daughter of Henry and Fanny Warren.

[87] *Lovell's Canadian Dominion Newfoundland Directory for 1871*, vol. 8 (Newfoundland), Montreal: John Lovell, 1871, shows John Warren, William Warren, sr, and William Warren, jr.

[88] *Baptisms, Marriages, Burials 1855-1872*, (Marriages) p. 32, #[60].

[89] Vital Records of NF, FHL film 2,168,731, Death Bk No. 10, p. 422, #31, old age, age 82.

[90] *Marriages, 1879-1896*, p. 68, #113, the son of William Warren.

[91] *Baptisms, Marriages, Burials, 1855-1872*, (Baptisms) p. 14, #337, the son of William and Frances Warren.

[92] *Marriages, 1879-1896*, p. 42, #70, the daughter of William Young. NF Census 1935, p. 426, living with William Warren, age 45, living next door to Wilson Warren, age 42.

[93] *Baptisms, Marriages, Burials, 1855-1872*, (Baptisms) p. 20, #470, the daughter of William and Frances.

Island.[94]

18. Emma Warren (John, Edward) was born February 1859 in Fox Island.[95] She married Ezekiel McDonald 17 September 1884 in Fox Island,[96] as his second wife, he having married first her twin sister, Mary Jane.

Ezekiel and Emma have the following children:

61 i. John Henry McDonald was born 27 September 1886 and christened 28 September 1886 in Fox Island.[97]

62 ii. Edward William McDonald was born 20 July 1887 and christened 28 July 1887 in Fox Island.[98]

63 iii. Elizabeth Jane McDonald was born 28 September 1890 and christened 9 October 1890 in Fox Island.[99]

64 iv. Edith Susannah McDonald was born 6 July 1893 and christened 16 August 1893 in Fox Island.[100]

65 v. John McDonald was born 26 March 1897 and christened 22 April 1897 in Fox Island.[101]

19. Susannah Warren (John, Edward) was born ca 1860 in Dog Cove. Susannah married John Bagg, son of Hugh Bagg, on 5 January 1893 in Dog Cove.[102] John was born ca 1837 in Bay de View.

John and Susannah have the following child:

66 i. James William Bagg was born 25 July 1894 in Dog Cove and was christened 14 September 1894 in Dog Cove.[103]

20. John Warren (John, Edward) was born ca 1861 in Fox Island. He died 12 July 1936 in Coppett.[104] John married Sarah Bagg 13 September 1892 in Dog Cove. Sarah was born ca

[94] *Baptisms, Marriages, Burials, 1855-1872*, (Baptisms) p. 23, #546, the daughter of William and Fanny Warren.

[95] NF Census 1921, p. 56.

[96] *Marriages, 1879-1896*, p. 33, #[55a], no ages given, no parents listed.

[97] *Baptisms, 1879-1893*, p. 47, #376, the actual dates of birth and baptism are reversed from those given in the text.

[98] *Baptisms, 1879-1893*, p. 55, #440.

[99] *Baptisms, 1879-1893*, p. 79, #627.

[100] *Baptisms, 1879-1893*, p. 1, #1.

[101] *Baptisms, 1879-1893*, p. 32, #253, son of Seigel and Emma McDonald.

[102] *Baptisms, Marriages, Burials, 1855-1872*, (Marriages p. 38, #[128]. Vital Records of NF, FHL film 2,168,994, Marriage Bk No. 2, p. 138, #3, witnesses: Hugh Bagg and Thomas Warren, groom stated to be widower, age 56. Marriage year given is 1892.

[103] *Baptisms, 1893-1905*, p. 9, #66.

[104] NF Census 1935, p. 428, age 75. Vital Records of NF, FHL film 2,168,733, Death Bk No. 12, p. 432, #23, age 76 yrs.

1868 in Dog Cove.[105] She died 6 December 1897 in Fox Island and was buried 8 December 1897 in Fox Island.[106]

John and Sarah have the following children:

> 67 i. John Bagg Warren was born 3 November 1894 in Fox Island and was christened 25 April 1895 in Fox Island.[107] He died 27 April 1896 in Fox Island and was buried in Fox Island.[108]
>
> 68 ii. George Edward Warren was born 7 March 1896 in Fox Island.[109] George married Susanna Bowles. Susanna was born about 1904.[110]

21. James Warren (John, Edward) was born August 1861 in Fox Island.[111] He died 23 September 1939 in Fox Island.[112] James married Susanna Warren, daughter of Henry Warren and Elizabeth Hayman, 19 September 1881 in Fox Island.[113] Susanna was christened 25 July 1867 in Fox Island.[114] She died 11 December 1898 in Fox Island and was buried 14 December 1898 in Fox Island.[115] See No. 38.

James and Susanna have the following children:

> 69 i. Arthur Francis Warren was born 21 October 1886 and was christened 23 October 1886 in Fox Island.[116]
>
> 70 ii. Samuel Edward Warren was born 22 December 1887 and was

---

[105] *Marriages, 1879-1896*, p. 94, #163, the son of John Warren. Vital Records of NF, FHL film 2,168,994, Marriage Bk No. 2, p. 136, #8.

[106] Vital Records of NF, FHL film 2,168,729, Death Bk No. 2, p. 230, #7, born Burgeo, died Fox Island, buried Dog Cove, age 29. *Burials, 1879-1912*, p. 47, #373..

[107] *Baptisms, 1893-1905*, p. 14, #107, parents are John and Sarah Warren, Fox Island, birth date given is 3 November 1894.

[108] Vital Records of NF, FHL film 2,168,729, Death Bk No. 2, p. 227, #1, born, died and buried Fox Island, age 1½ yrs.

[109] *Baptisms, 1893-1905*, p. 24, #190. Vital Records of NF, FHL film 2,168,999, Birth Bk No. 3, p. 338, #31. NF Census 1935, p. 428, age 39, wife Susanna, living with father-in-law, John Warren, age 75, and Nathan G. Bowles, brother-in-law.

[110] NF Census 1935, p. 428, age 31.

[111] NF Census 1921, p. 50, James, widower, age 60, born Fox Island, August 1861, living with his aunt, Jane Warren, age 70, born Ramea. NF Census 1935, p. 431, age 82 (birth 1853), living with son, Samuel Edward, age 48, and daughter-in-law, Elizabeth Frances Warren, age 42.

[112] Vital Records of NF, FHL film 2,168,733, Death Bk No. 13, p. 432, #28, age 79 yrs. There are two Warren men named James in *McAlpine Newfoundland Directory for 1904*, entry for Fox Island: James (son of John), and James, sr. This James is identified with James , sr, in 1904, while James, the son of John, is the son of John Albert Warren (known as John all his life).

[113] *Marriage, 1879-1896*, p. 16, #31, the son of John Warren.

[114] *Baptisms, Marriages, Burials, 1855-1872*, (Baptisms) p. 21, #499, the daughter of Henry and Elizabeth Warren.

[115] *Burials 1879-1912*, p. 55, #433.

[116] *Baptisms, 1879-1893*, p. 47, #375, the son of James and Susan Warren.

christened 9 April 1888 in Fox Island.[117] He died October 1940 in Fox Island.[118] Samuel married Elizabeth Frances (---). She was born ca 1893.[119]

71   iii.   John Francis Warren was born 27 September 1890 and was christened October 1890 in Fox Island.[120] He died 25 May 1899 in Fox Island and was buried 27 May 1899 in Fox Island.[121]

72   iv.   Miriam Jane Warren was christened 12 September 1892 in Fox Island.[122] She died 5 April 1893 in Fox Island and was buried 8 April 1893 in Fox Island.[123]

73   v.   Mary Anne Warren was born 4 February 1894 in Fox Island.[124]

22. Thomas Warren (John, Edward) was born June 1863 in Little River.[125] Thomas married Elizabeth (---) before 1882. Elizabeth was born ca 1861.

Thomas and Elizabeth have the following children:

74   i.   Thomas William Warren was born 7 July 1882 and was christened 28 August 1882 in Little River.[126] Thomas married Elenor Dominey 4 October 1907 in Little River.[127] Elenor was born ca 1891 in Little River.

75   ii.   Frances Jane Warren was born 26 May 1884 and was christened 19 August 1884 in Little River.[128]

76   iii.   Frances Jane Warren was christened 16 August 1885 in Little River.[129]

---

[117]   *Baptisms, 1879-1893*, p. 61, #482, the son of James and Susanna Warren. NF Census 1921, p. 54, born December 1886 (Fox Island), wife Elizabeth F. Warren, born August 1892 (Fox Island), and children: Susannah, born August 1912 (Fox Island), Dinah, born August 1914 (Fox Island), James W., born August 1917 (Fox Island), and Gladys, born June 1920 (Fox Island).

[118]   Vital Records of NF, FHL film 2,168,733, Death Bk No. 13, p. 434, #38, drowned at sea, age 52, No date given for death but found between October and November dates 1940.

[119]   NF Census 1935, p. 431, age 42.

[120]   *Baptisms, 1879-1893*, p. 79, #626, the son of James and Susanna Warren.

[121]   *Burials, 1879-1912*, p. 79, #436. Vital Records of NF, FHL film 2,168,727, Death Bk No. 3, p. 374, #5.

[122]   *Baptisms, 1879-1893*, p. 93, #744, the daughter of James and Susanna Warren.

[123]   *Burials, 1879-1912*, p. 23, #271. Vital Records of NF, FHL film 2,168,729, Death Bk No. 2, p. 138, #35, born, died, and buried Fox Island, age 7 mos.

[124]   Vital Records of NF, FHL film 2,168,999, Birth Bk No. 3, p. 486, #18, parents are James and Susannah Warren.

[125]   NF Census 1921, p. 12.

[126]   *Baptisms, 1879-1893*, p. 26, #202, the son of Thomas and Elizabeth Warren. NF Census 1921, p. 12, spouse Charlotte, born 1881, older man (father), Thomas, born 1863.

[127]   Vital Records of NF, FHL film 2,168,996, Marriage Bk No. 5, p. 384, #7.

[128]   *Baptisms, 1879-1893*, p. 36, #288, the daughter of Thomas and Elizabeth Warren.

[129]   *Baptisms, 1879-1893*, p. 343 #340, the daughter of Thomas and Elizabeth Warren.

23. Ann Warren (John, Edward) was born 28 May 1862 in Little River.[130] She married William Vardy 6 March 1886 in Burgeo.[131] William was born ca 1850 at Bonne Bay[132] and died 14 February 1928 in Fox Island.[133]

William and Ann have the following children:

77 i.   Elizabeth Jane Vardy was christened 12 April 1886 in Burgeo.[134]

78 ii.   John William Vardy was born 13 August 1887 and was christened the same day in Fox Island.[135] He married Lucy Maud McDonald 16 November 1910 in Fox Island.[136]

79 iii.   Louisa Vardy was born 18 April 1889 and christened 30 April 1889 in Fox Island.[137] She married Michael Carroll 21 August 1907 in Burgeo.[138]

80 iv.   Mary Vardy was born 29 May 1891 and christened 15 June 1891 in Fox Island.[139] She married Joseph Cole(y) 15 August 1907 in Fox Island.[140] See No. 99.

81 v.   George Albert Vardy was born 30 June 1893 and christened 15 August 1893 in Fox Island.[141] He married Hannah Jane Hayman 7 September 1916 in Fox Island.[142] She died 19 June 1936 in Fox Island.[143]

82 vi.   Edward Francis Vardy was born 20 July 1895 and christened that day in Fox Island.[144]

83 vii.   Florence Vardy was born 23 November 1897 and christened 26 November 1897 in Fox Island.[145] She died (named Flora in the

---

[130] Internet: <<http://www.chebuckto.ns.ca/Heritage/NGB/Parish/>>, Fortune – Belleoram, Church of England Baptisms 1846-1866, downloaded copy in possession of the author, states christening was at Facheau. NF census 1921, p. 54. The birthplace (Burgeo) listed in the latter two sources for Annie Vardy and two of her children seem to be incorrect.

[131] *Marriages, 1879-1896.* p. 41, #69, the son of William Vardy, the daughter of John Warren.

[132] NF Census 1921, p. 54. The census listing shows a birthplace for William of Sherbourne, England.

[133] Vital Records of NF, FHL film 2,168,727, Death Bk No. 10, p. 424, #11, age 78 yrs.

[134] *Baptisms, 1879-1893*, p. 47, #374.

[135] *Baptisms, 1879-1893*, p. 55, #439.

[136] Vital Records of NF, FHL film 2,168,996, Marriage Bk No. 6, p. 387, #8, she is 20 and he is 23. See also Bk 6, p 395, #13, gives full name of bride, same ages.

[137] *Baptisms, 1879-1893*, p. 68, #544.

[138] Vital Records of NF, FHL film 2,168,996, Marriage Bk No. 5, p. 382, #11, she is 18 and he is 24.

[139] *Baptisms, 1879-1893*, p. 83, #664.

[140] Vital Records of NF, FHL film 2,168,996, Marriage Bk No. 5, p. 385, #1, she is 22 and he is 24.

[141] *Baptisms, 1879-1893*, p. 100, #800.

[142] Vital Records of NF, FHL film 2,168,996, Marriage Bk No. 7, p. 395, #11, she is 17 and he is 23. His name is given as George Alf Vardy.

[143] Vital Records of NF, FHL film 2,168,727, Death Bk No. 12, p. 425, #11, age 34 yrs.

[144] *Baptisms, 1879-1893*, p. 17, #136.

[145] *Baptisms, 1879-1893*, p. 39, #311. Vital Records of NF, FHL film 2,168,999, Birth Bk No. 3, p. 349, #35.

record) 5 June 1902 in Fox Island, age 6.[146]

84   viii.   Violet May Vardy was born 6 August 1903 and christened 13 September 1903 in Fox Island.[147] She married John William Bunter 12 November 1918 in Fox Island.[148]

27. George Warren (John, Edward) was born May 1875 in Fox Island.[149] George married Fanny Rose 13 July 1901 at Grey River.[150] Fanny was born August 1881.[151]

George and Fanny have the following children:

85   i.   Elizabeth Jane Warren was born 17 April 1902 and christened 19 April 1902 in Fox Island.[152]

86   ii.   Sarah Warren was born October 1905 in Fox Island.[153]

87   iii.   Susy Warren was born November 1909 in Fox Island.[154]

88   iv.   Lucy Warren was born December 1910 in Fox Island.[155]

89   v.   John William Warren was born 9 January 1921 and christened 17 January 1921 in Fox Island.[156]

28. Elizabeth Warren (Bavillam, Edward) was born March 1850 in Fox Island.[157] Elizabeth married William Cole 28 December 1868 in Fox Island.[158] William was born ca 1844 in Hunt's Island.[159] He died 23 October 1899 and was buried 26 October 1899 at Fox Island, aged 64 years.[160] Elizabeth died 22 September 1940, at Fox Island.[161]

William and Elizabeth had the following children:

90   i.   William Cole was christened 10 April 1870 in Lower Burgeo.[162]

[146]   Vital Records of NF, FHL film 2,168,727, Death Bk No. 3, p. 381, #24.

[147]   *Baptisms, 1879-1893*, p. 82, #653.

[148]   Vital Records of NF, FHL film 2,168,997, Marriage Bk No. 8, , p. 400, #12, she is 15 and he is 18.

[149]   NF Census 1921, p. 55.

[150]   *Marriages, 1896-1906*, p. 31, #60, he was 26, the son of John Warren, she was 21.

[151]   NF Census 1921, p. 55.

[152]   *Baptisms, 1893-1906*, p. 71, #566, the daughter of George and Fanny Warren. NF Census 1921, p. 55.

[153]   NF Census 1921, p. 55.

[154]   NF Census 1921, p. 55.

[155]   NF Census 1921, p. 55.

[156]   *Baptisms, 1917-1943*, p. 21, #162, the son of George and Fanny Warren.

[157]   NF Census 1921, p. 52A, listed as Elizabeth Coley, widow, age 71, born Mar 1850, living with James A. Coley, son of William and Elizabeth Coley.

[158]   She married William Cole, a widower, who had previously married Rachel Harris. Rachel died at age 24 in 1867 (born 1843). *Baptisms, Marriages, Burials 1855-1872*, (Marriages) p. 35, #'95', first marriage, Rachel Harris.

[159]   *Baptisms, Marriages, Burials 1855-1872*, (Marriages) p. 35, #'95', first marriage, Rachel Harris.

[160]   *Burials 1879-1912*, p. 55, #439.

[161]   Vital Records of NF, FHL film 2,168,733, Death Bk No. 13, p. 434, #9.

[162]   *Baptisms, Marriages, Burials 1855-1872*, (Baptisms) p. 25, #586, the son of William and Elizabeth Cole.

91 ii. John Cole was born November 1870 at Burgeo.[163] He married Sarah (---) who was born February 1884.[164] Sarah died 25 February 1937 in Fox Island.[165] John died 6 January 1945 at Fox Island.[166]

92 iii. Samuel Cole was born ca 1872 in Fox Island. He married Elizabeth Warren, the daughter of Edward Warren and Jane Rose, 6 September 1897 at Fox Island.[167] He died 1 June 1926 in Fox Island.[168] See No. 49.

93 iv. Edith Jane Cole was born ca 1873 in Fox Island. She married John Hayman 25 September 1889 in Fox Island.[169] John was born ca 1866.

94 v. Emma Cole was born ca 1875 in Fox Island. She married Abraham Hayman 13 September 1894 in Fox Island.[170]

95 vi. Thomas Cole was born ca 1878 in Fox Island and married Bridget Bowles 29 July 1903 at Fox Island.[171] Bridget died 12 October 1919.[172]

96 vii. Reuben Cole was christened 9 May 1884 (named Colley) probably in Fox Island.[173] He married Susan Harvey 29 August 1901 at Fox Island.[174]

97 viii. Joseph Henry Cole was born 24 February 1884 in Fox Island and was christened 9 May 1884 in Fox Island.[175] He married Mary Vardy 15 August 1907 in Fox Island.[176] See No. 82.

98 ix. Philip Arthur Cole was born 19 April 1887 and was christened 4

---

[163] NF Census 1921, p. 52A.

[164] NF Census 1921, p. 52A.

[165] Vital Records of NF, FHL film 2,168,733, Death Bk No. 12, p. 433, #22. She was age 50.

[166] Vital Records of NF, FHL film 2,168,733, Individual Death Certificates, #104342, age 75.

[167] *Marriages, 1879-1896*, p. 3, #5, age 25, son of William Coley, she is age 25, daughter of Edward Warren. Thomas Coley is a witness.

[168] Vital Records of NF, FHL film 2,168,730, Death Bk No. 9, p. 441, #9. He was age 45.

[169] *Marriages, 1879-1896*, p. 70, #[116], the son of Benj.

[170] *Marriages, 1879-1896*, p. 109, #[192], age 19, the daughter of William Coley. He was age 26, the son of Benjamin Hayman.

[171] *Marriages 1896-1906*, p. 46, #90, age 25, the son of William Coley, she is 17, daughter of Frank Bowles.

[172] Vital Records of NF, FHL film 2,168,730, Death Bk No. 8, p. 400, #33. She was age 33.

[173] *Baptisms, 1879-1893*, p. 35, #273, the son of William and Elizabeth Cole. NF Census 1921, p. 53, Reuben Cole is listed with wife Susan (born January 1881 – Isle aux Morts), and children: William (born August 1902), Julia (born July 1906), John (born January 1909), and Sandy (born October 1912). All the children were born in Fox Island.

[174] *Marriages 1896-1906*, p. 32, #62, age 21, son of William Coley, she is age 20, the daughter of William Harvey.

[175] *Baptisms, 1879-1893*, p. 35, #273, the son of William and Elizabeth Cole. NF Census 1921, p. 52A, Arthur Coley is listed with his wife, Minnie (born June 1896 at Fox Island), and children: George W. (born August 1917) and Emily J. (born August 1920). All the children were born at Fox Island.

[176] Vital Records of NF, FHL film 2,168,996, Marriage Bk No. 7, p. 385, #1, Joseph is age 24 and Mary is 22.

May 1887 in Fox Island.[177] He married Minnie Bunter 2 December 1913 in Fox Island.[178]

99　x.　Grace Cole was born 9 June 1889 and christened 22 June 1889 in Fox Island.[179] Grace married Benjamin Hayman 15 August 1907 at Fox Island.[180]

100　xi.　James Albert Cole was born 26 December 1893 in Fox Island.[181] He married Elsie Eavis 2 December 1922 at Fox Island.[182]

30. Thomas Warren (Bavillam, Edward) was born ca 1855. He died 2 October 1910 and was buried 5 December 1910 in Bay de View.[183] Thomas married first Mary Ann (---), who was born ca 1869. She subsequently married Hubert Rose 9 September 1895 at Fox Island.[184]
Thomas and Mary Ann have the following children:

101　i.　Edith Jane Warren was christened 4 June 1880 in Fox Island.[185]

102　ii.　Elizabeth Warren was born 16 October 1883 and christened 9 May 1884 in Fox Island.[186]

103　iii.　John William Warren was born 1 April 1888 and was christened 9 April 1888 in Fox Island.[187] He died 5 June 1906 at Fox Island.[188]

104　iv.　Henry Warren was born 1 April 1888 and christened 9 April 1888 in Fox Island.[189] Henry married Rebecca Hayman 3 October 1910

---

[177]　*Baptisms, 1879-1893*, p. 53, #422, the son of William and Elizabeth Cole. NF Census 1921, p. 52A, Arthur Coley is listed with his wife, Minnie (b June 1896 at Fox Island), and children: George W. (born August 1917) and Emily J. (born August 1920). All the children were born at Fox Island.

[178]　Vital Records of NF, FHL film 2,168,996, Marriage Bk No. 7, p. 384, #9, Arthur is age 26 and Minnie is 17.

[179]　*Baptisms, 1879-1893*, p. 70, #558, the daughter of William and Elizabeth Cole.

[180]　Vital Records of NF, FHL film 2,168,996, Marriage Bk No. 5, p. 384, #15, Benjamin is age 25 and Grace is 21.

[181]　Vital Records of NF, FHL film 2,168,733, Birth Bk No. 2, p. 278, #21, son of William and Elizabeth Coley, born Fox Island. NF Census 1921, p. 52A, age 26, born December 1894, single.

[182]　Vital Records of NF, FHL film 2,168,997, Marriage Bk No. 9, p. 305, #4. James is age 28 and Elsie is 19.

[183]　Vital Records of NF, FHL film 2,168,728, Death Bk No. 5, p. 403, #40, died of consumption at Bay de View, born and buried Fox Island, age 55 yrs. *Burials, 1879-1912*, p. 95, #760, age 55 yrs.

[184]　Vital Records of NF, FHL film 2,168,994, Marriage Bk No. 2, p. 208, #9, age 22, widow.

[185]　*Baptisms, 1879-1893*, p. 9, #69, the daughter of Thomas and Mary Ann Warren.

[186]　*Baptisms, 1879-1893*, p. 35, #276, the daughter of Thomas and Mary Ann Warren.

[187]　*Baptisms, 1879-1893*, p. 61, #61, the son of Thomas and Mary Ann Warren.

[188]　Vital Records of NF, FHL film 2,168,728, Death Bk No. 5, p. 414, #20, of consumption, age 18, born and buried at Fox Island.

[189]　*Baptisms, 1879-1893*, p. 61, #481, the son of Thomas and Mary Ann Warren. NF Census 1921, p. 53, shows Henry with wife Rebecca Warren, born November 1887 (Fox Island) and two children, Bessy, born September 1912 (Fox Island), and Sarah, born October 1919 (Fox Island).

in Fox Island.[190] Rebecca was born ca 1888 in Fox Island.

105 v.   Frances Warren was born 10 October 1892 and was christened 21 October 1892 in Fox Island.[191] She died 6 April 1893 and was buried in Fox Island.[192]

31.[193] William Warren (Bavillam, Edward) was born about 1858. William Married Susanna (---) before 1880 in Little River. Susanna was born ca 1859 in Little River.[194] She died 4 July 1859 in Burgeo.[195]

William and Susanna have these children:

106 i.   Susanna J. Warren was christened 2 June 1880 in Little River.[196] She married John Stickland 11 October 1899 in Burgeo.[197] John was born ca 1878.

107 ii.   William Warren was born 1 October 1881 in Little River and christened there 26 August 1882. He died in 1968.[198] William married Sarah Keeping 19 September 1906 in Ramea.[199] She was born ca 1887 and died 10 September 1976 at Ramea.[200]

108 iii.   Matthew Warren was christened 2 July 1883 in Little River.[201] He

---

[190]   Vital Records of NF, FHL film 2,168,996, Marriage Bk No. 5, p. 386, #2,.

[191]   *Baptisms, 1879-1893*, p. 95, #756, the daughter of Thomas and Mary Ann Warren.

[192]   Vital Records of NF, FHL film 2,168,729, Death Bk 2, p. 138, #36, born, died, and buried at Fox Island, age 6 mos. May be mistaken for Jessie Frances Warren, daughter of Thomas and Mary Ann.

[193]   William M. Litchman, "Shaving with Occam's Razor: A Proposed Descendancy for Edward Warren of Fox Island, Newfoundland, Part III, *The Newfoundland Ancestor*, Vol 18, #2, Spring 2002, pp. 65-74.

[194]   NF Census 1921, p. 117, shows Susan Warren, b September 1859, Grey (Little) River, widow, living in Burgeo. NF Census 1935, p. 472, age 79, living with Thomas Taylor, age 66.

[195]   Vital Records of NF, FHL film 2,168,733, Death Bk No. 12, p. 426, #10, senilit, age 75 (born ca 1861, Little River).

[196]   *Baptisms, 1879-1893*, p. 9, #67, the daughter of William and Susanna Warren.

[197]   Vital Records of NF, FHL film 2,168,995, Marriage Bk No. 3, p. 392, #15, groom age 21, Susanna J. age 19.

[198]   *Baptisms, 1879-1893*, p. 26, #201, the son of William and Susanna Warren. NF Census 1921, p. 90, born September 1880 (Little River), wife Sarah, born June 1887 (Ramea), children: John, born March 1909 (Ramea, Dora, born February 1911 (Ramea), Wilson, born May 1913 (Ramea), Susannah, born May 1913 (Ramea), and Garland, born November 1916 (Ramea). Victor G. Kendall and Victor Kendall, *Ramea's Family Tree*, Corner Brook (NF): Victor G. and Victor Kendall, 1995, says he is the second child (of three) of William and Susanna Warren (of Little River. NF Census 1935, p. 438.

[199]   Mentioned in Victor G. Kendall and Victor Kendall, *Ramea's Family Tree*, Corner Brook (NF): Victor G. and Victor Kendall, 1995. NF Census 1935, p. 438. Vital Records of NF, FHL film 2,168, 996, Marriage Bk No. 5, p. 379, #13.

[200]   Obituary for Sarah Keeping Warren is available on the internet at the Newfoundland GenWeb site under Gulf News Obits, 1976.

[201]   *Baptisms, 1879-1893*, p. 26, #201, the son of William and Susanna Warren. NF Census 1921, p. 92, born July 1883 (Little River), wife, Eva, born June 1888 (Red Island), children: William, born February 1907 (Red Island), Elizabeth, born June 1909 (Red Island), Laura, born August 1911 (Burgeo), Norman, born August 1913

married Eva Swift 2 September 1905 in Red Island.[202] Eva was born ca 1888 in Red Island.

34. **Edward Warren** (Henry, Edward) was born ca 1855.[203] Edward married first Frances (---) before 1879. Frances was born ca 1858. She was buried 31 January 1891 in Fox Island.[204] They have children:

> 109 i. Susannah Warren was christened 17 August 1879 in Fox Island.[205] Susannah married William Robert Kendall 23 October 1897 in Ramea.[206] William was born ca 1875 in Ramea.
>
> 110 ii. Mary Jane Warren was born 13 September 1881 and was christened 19 September 1881, all in Fox Island.[207] Mary married William Kendall 21 April 1900 in Ramea.[208] William was born ca 1881.
>
> 111 iii. John Henry Warren was born 11 April 1884 and christened 9 May 1884 at Fox Island.[209]
>
> 112 iv. George Samuel Warren was born 9 July 1886 and christened 18 July 1886 in Fox Island.[210] George married Elizabeth J. McDonald 8 September 1908 in Fox Island.[211] Elizabeth was born ca 1890 in Fox Island.
>
> 113 v. Sarah Frances Warren was born 22 August 1888 and christened 21 September 1888 in Fox Island.[212]
>
> 114 vi. Elizabeth Warren was born 27 January 1891 and christened 28 Jan 1891 in Fox Island.[213] Elizabeth married Mark Bolt before 1920.

(Burgeo), Matthew, born January 1917 (Burgeo), and Violet, born June 1921 (Burgeo).

[202] Vital Records of NF, FHL film 2,168,995, Marriage Bk No. 4, p. 396, #5. NF Census 1935, p. 500.

[203] *McAlpine Newfoundland Directory for 1898*, entry for Fox Island, shows Edward

[204] *Burials, 1879-1912*, p. 29, #226.

[205] *Baptisms, 1879-1893*, p. 5, #34, the daughter of Edward and Frances Warren.

[206] *Marriages, 1879-1896*, p. 4, #8. Vital Records of NF, FHL film 2,168,995, Marriage Bk No. 3, p. 387, #12.

[207] *Baptisms, 1879-1893*, p. 20, #160, the daughter of Edward and Frances Warren.

[208] Vital Records of NF, FHL film 2,168,995, Marriage Bk No. 3, p. 395, #10, age 19.

[209] *Baptisms, 1879-1893*, p. 35, #275, the son of Edward and Frances Warren.

[210] *Baptisms, 1879-1893*, p. 49, #390, the son of Edward and Frances Warren. NF Census 1921, p. 55, born December 1885 (Fox Island), wife Elizabeth, born September 1890 (Fox Island), children: Susannah, born January 1910 (Fox Island), John, born November 1911 (Fox Island), Emmanuel, born September 1915 (Fox Island), and Edgaqr, born September 1918 (Fox Island). NF Census 1935, p. 435, age 56.

[211] Vital Records of NF, FHL film 2,168,996, Marriage Bk No. 5, p. 387, #8. NF Census 1835m o, 435, age 46,

[212] *Baptisms, 1879-1893*, p. 65, #516, the daughter of Edward and Frances Warren.

[213] *Baptisms, 1879-1893*, p. 84, #669, the daughter of Edward and Frances Warren. Elizabeth (age 39) is listed with Mark Bolt in NF Census 1935, and his father-in-law, Edwarren, age 80.

Mark was born ca 1889.[214]

Edward married second Barthena Niel 21 August 1891 in West Cul de Sac.[215] She died 23 September 1914 at Bay de View.[216] Edward and Barthena have these children:

115 vii.   Elizabeth Louisa Warren was christened 31 December 1893 in Cul de Sac.[217]

116 viii. Harriett Warren was born 23 November 1897 and christened 30 November 1897 in Cul de Sac[218]. Harriett married Francis Lushman 26 August 1915 in Grey River.[219] She died 20 June 1916 in Grey River.[220]

36. Hannah Warren (Henry, Edward) was born ca 1858 in Burgeo. She married George William Matthews 9 May 1879 in Burgeo.[221] George was born ca 1855 in Burgeo.

George and Hannah have the following children:

117 i.   Henry Matthews was christened 31 August 1880 in Burgeo.[222] He was buried 28 September 1880 in Burgeo.[223]

118 ii.   Joseph Strange Matthews was born 5 May 1882 and was christened 9 July 1882 in Burgeo.[224] He was buried 9 July 1883 in Burgeo.[225]

119 iii.   Henrietta Matthews was christened 4 May 1884 in Burgeo.[226]

120 iv.   Maude Matthews was born 8 December 1885 and christened 22 December 1885 in Burgeo.[227]

121 v.   Elizabeth Matthews was born 2 October 1890 and christened 30 November 1890 in Burgeo.[228]

122 vi.   Edwin Matthews was born 15 March 1893 and christened 21 May

---

[214]   NF Census 1935, p. 185.

[215]   Vital Records of NF, FHL film 2,168,994, Marriage Bk No. 1, p. 35, #17. This record is found with others of Fortune Bay.

[216]   Vital Records of NF, FHL film 2,168,729, Death Bk No. 6, p. 411, #19, age 53 yrs.

[217]   Vital Records of NF, FHL film 2,168,995, Birth Bk No. 1,.

[218]   Vital Records of NF, FHL film 2,168,995, Birth Bk No. 1, 2,.

[219]   Vital Records of NF, FHL film 2,168,995, Marriage Bk No. 7, p. 391, #12.

[220]   Vital Records of NF, FHL film 2,168,729, Death Bk No. 7, p. 395, #17, age 18 yrs.

[221]   *Marriages, 1879-1896*, p. 8, #15, groom the son of Jno. Matthews, bride the daughter of Henry Warren.

[222]   *Baptisms, 1879-1893*, p. 25, #195, the son of George and Hannah Matthews.

[223]   *Burials, 1879-1912*, p. 2, #14.

[224]   *Baptisms, 1879-1893*, p. 25, #195, the son of George and Hannah Matthews.

[225]   *Burials, 1879-1912*, p. 6, #48.

[226]   *Baptisms, 1879-1893*, p. 34, #272, the daughter of George and Hannah Matthews.

[227]   *Baptisms, 1879-1893*, p. 46, #363, the daughter of George and Hannah Matthews.

[228]   *Baptisms, 1879-1893*, p. 81, #644, the daughter of George and Hannah Matthews.

1893 in Burgeo.[229]

123 vii.   John Matthews was born 27 September 1895 and christened 29 November 1895 in Burgeo.[230]

124 viii.   George William Matthews was born 21 April 1898 and christened 19 June 1898 at Collier's Island.[231]

39. Susanna Warren (Henry, Edward) married James Warren, son of John Warren and Elizabeth. See No. 21.

40. Elizabeth Warren (Henry, Edward) was christened 20 May 1870 in Fox Island.[232] She died 24 July 1918 in Fox Island.[233] She married Edward William Warren, son of Edward Warren and Jane Rose, 5 December 1887 in Fox Island.[234] See No. 45.

    Edward and Elizabeth have the following children:

125 i.   Elwood Warren was born 15 July 1889 and christened 16 July in Fox Island.[235]

126 ii.   Menira Frances Warren was born 15 October 1892 and christened 21 October 1892 in Fox Island.[236]

127 iii.   Henry Edward Warren was born 23 January 1894 in Fox Island.[237] Henry married Mary Ann (---).[238]

128 iv.   Arthur Thomas Warren was born 28 September 1896 and christened 17 October 1896 in Fox Island.[239]

43. Albert John Warren (Thomas, Edward) was born June 1858 in Fox Island.[240] Albert married Grace (---).

    Albert John and Grace had the following children.

---

[229]   *Baptisms, 1879-1893*, p. 99, #786, the son of George and Hannah Matthews.

[230]   *Baptisms, 1879-1893*, p. 19, #149, the son of George and Hannah Matthews.

[231]   *Baptisms, 1879-1893*, p. 39, #310, the son of George and Hannah Matthews.

[232]   *Baptisms, 1879-1893*, p. 26, #608, the daughter of Henry and Elizabeth Warren.

[233]   Vital Records of NF, FHL film 2,268,729, Death Bk No. .7, p. 403, #35, of consumption, age 49.

[234]   *Marriages, 1879-1896*, p. 57, #[96], the daughter of Henry Warren.

[235]   *Baptisms, 1879-1893*, p. 70, #557, the son of Edward and Elizabeth Warren.

[236]   *Baptisms, 1879-1893*, p. 95, #755, the daughter of Edward and Elizabeth Warren.

[237]   Vital Records of NF, FHL film 2,168,999, Birth Bk No. 2, p. 486, #17, parents are Edward and Elizabeth Warren, born Fox Island. NF Census 19335, p. 434, age 40, with wife and many children, and father, Edward, age 73.

[238]   NF Census 1935, p. 434.

[239]   Vital Records of NF, FHL film 2,168,999, Birth Bk No. 3, p. 340, #24.

[240]   NF Census 1921, p. 52A, shows John Warren, born June 1858 (Fox Island). Names Albert John in birth record for Barzilla Albert Warren. *Baptisms, 1879-1893*, p. 75, #595. Known as John throughout his life.

129 i.   Elizabeth Warren was christened 17 August 1879 in Fox Island.[241]

130 ii.   Brazillia Albert Warren was christened 28 May 1881 in Fox Island.[242]

131 iii.   James William Warren was born 7 September 1883 and christened 13 September 1883 in Fox Island.[243] James married Hannah Bowles 3 September 1906 in Little River.[244] Hannah was born ca 1886 in Coppett.

132 iv.   John Warren was born 10 October 1889 and christened 18 October 1889 in Fox Island.[245]

133 v.   Susanna Warren was christened 7 July 1892 in Fox Island.[246]

44. Isabella Warren (Thomas, Edward) was christened 3 June 1861 in Ramea.[247] She was buried 13 January 1893 in Burgeo.[248] Isabella married John Bungay in 1886 in Burgeo.[249] John was born ca 1862 in Burgeo. He died ca 1921.[250]

John and Isabella have the following children:

134 i.   Helen Bungay was born 25 January 1889 and christened 3 February 1889 in Burgeo.[251] She was buried on 3 May 1889 in Burgeo.[252]

135 ii.   Annabelle Bungay was born 6 April 1890 and christened 6 July 1890 in Burgeo.[253]

---

[241]   *Baptisms, 1879-1893*, p. 4, #32, the daughter of John and Grace.

[242]   *Baptisms, 1879-1893*, p. 17, #130, the son of John and Grace. NF Census 1821, p. 56 shows Albert Warren, born January 1881 (Fox Island), living with John Warren, born Ocxt 1889 (Fox Island) [brothers]. Birth record names father as Albert John Warren. NF Census 1935, p. 430, with brother, John.

[243]   *Baptisms, 1879-1893*, p. 32, #252, the son of John and Grace. NF Census 1821, p. 53 shows James with wife Hannah Warren, born April 1888 (Coppett), and children: Leah, born November 1908 (Fox Island),m Edna, born May 1910 (Fox Island), Alice, born December 1912 (Fox Island), John F., born February 1915 (Fox Island), and Susy, born March 1917 (Fox Island). In NF Census 1935, p. 435, age 52, widower with many children.

[244]   Vital Records of NF, FHL film 2,168,996, Marriage Bk No. 5, p. 379, #11.

[245]   *Baptisms, 1879-1893*, p. 75, #595, the son of John and Grace Warren. NF Census 1821, p. 56 shows Albert Warren, born January 1881 (Fox Island), living with John Warren, born October 1889 (Fox Island) [brothers]. NF Census 1935, p. 430, with brother "Albert."

[246]   *Baptisms, 1879-1893*, p. 92, #729, the daughter of John and Grace Warren.

[247]   *Baptisms, Marriages, Burials, 1855-1872*, (Baptisms) p. 9, #212, the daughter of Thomas and Sarah Warren.

[248]   *Burials, 1879-1912*, p. 33, #260.

[249]   *Marriages, 1879-1896*, p. 45, #74, the daughter of Thomas Warren. No month or day readable.

[250]   Death year given by Joseph Small in his "Diary." He also mentions that after his wife died, he went west and married a widow.

[251]   *Baptisms, 1879-1893*, p. 67, #635, the daughter of John and Isabella Bungay.

[252]   *Burials, 1879-1912*, p. 23, #183

[253]   *Baptisms, 1879-1893*, p. 77, #610, the daughter of John and Isabella Bungay.

45. Edward William Warren (Edward, Edward) married Elizabeth Warren, daughter of Henry Warren and Elizabeth Hayman. See No. 40.

www.ingramcontent.com/pod-product-compliance
Lightning Source LLC
Chambersburg PA
CBHW081646280326
41928CB00069B/3100